Notes on
English Literature

THE PRELUDE
I & II

W. Graham

BASIL BLACKWELL

© Basil Blackwell 1968

First published 1968

Reprinted 1983

ISBN 0 631 97770 8

Printed and bound in Great Britain by
Whitstable Litho Ltd., Whitstable, Kent.

CONTENTS

GENERAL NOTE

This series of introductions to the great classics of English literature is designed primarily for the school, college, and university student, although it is hoped that they will be found helpful by a much larger audience. Three aims have been kept in mind:

(A) To give the reader the relevant information necessary for his fuller understanding of the work.

(B) To indicate the main areas of critical interest, to suggest suitable critical approaches, and to point out possible critical difficulties.

(C) To do this in as simple and lucid a manner as possible, avoiding technical jargon and giving a full explanation of any critical terms employed.

Each introduction contains questions on the text and suggestions for further reading. It should be emphasized that in no sense is any introduction to be considered as a substitute for the reader's own study, understanding, and appreciation of the work.

AUTHOR'S NOTE

All quotations from Books I and II of *The Prelude* are taken from: *Wordsworth. The Prelude. Books I, II, and parts of V and XII*, edited by Helen Darbishire (Oxford University Press). This is a useful schools edition which prints appropriate extracts from the 1805 text for purposes of comparison. All other quotations from Wordsworth are taken from: *The Poetical Works of William Wordsworth*, edited by Thomas Hutchinson (Oxford University Press).

Discussion of *Tintern Abbey* and *Ode: Intimations of Immortality* is not intended to be full; I have limited it to such aspects of those poems as may illuminate the first two books of *The Prelude*.

EGOTISTICAL OR SUBLIME?

1 *Biographical and Critical*

'It was', said Wordsworth, 'a thing unprecedented in literary history that a man should talk so much about himself.' While Wordsworth's frank admission disarms criticism, there is a grain of truth in it which has proved unpalatable to a number of readers. Keats, notably, found the 'wordsworthian or egotistical sublime' alien to his poetic temperament, though his letters give evidence of his admiration for Wordsworth's poetry. I do not think that the question of Wordsworth's egotism need trouble us much. *The Prelude* was not designed for publication in Wordsworth's own life-time; it is arguably the most private of his poems, intended partly for the ear of his close friend and collaborator Coleridge and partly as an aid to his own spiritual exploration and development. 'It is not', he wrote to Sir George Beaumont, 'self-conceit that has induced me to do this, but real humility. I began the work because I was unprepared to treat any more arduous subject, and diffident of my own powers.'

Yet it remains true that *The Prelude* is 'unprecedented in literary history' and that it is 'about himself'. If we ask ourselves why this is so, I think we shall find that the answers lie partly in Wordsworth's historical position in English literature and partly in his personal biography. The two overlap, of course, but it may be desirable at this point to distinguish some of the more important features of Wordsworth's life, of what we might call his 'outer' biography. For his 'inner' life, the 'Growth of a

Poet's Mind', we must go to *The Prelude* itself; the distinction is a valuable and necessary one.

Wordsworth was born at Cockermouth in Cumberland in 1770. He had three brothers, and an only sister, Dorothy, a year younger than himself. His mother died when he was only eight and he was sent in the following year to the Grammar School at Hawkshead, where he boarded, together with other boys, in the cottage of Ann Tyson. The living was frugal but the life a happy, vigorous, out-door one and Wordsworth never forgot its influence. His father, who was agent to Lord Lowther, died in 1783, when Wordsworth was only thirteen. The consequences for the family were considerable; his financial affairs were in confusion and the children spent many years trying to regain an inheritance which was rightfully theirs. They were left in the guardianship of uncles, though Wordsworth spent most of his time with his mother's parents in Penrith, where he found the atmosphere irksome and restricting; Dorothy went to another branch of the family and for a long time they scarcely met.

In 1787 he went up to St. John's College, Cambridge, where he chafed at the academic studies but read widely in literature of his own choosing. On graduating in 1791, he resisted the pressure put upon him by his uncles to enter the Church or take up law and for several years the apparent aimlessness of his career was a source of disappointment to family and friends, though we can see now that Wordsworth was unconsciously fitting himself to be a poet by acquiring experience of the world at large. Of this experience the most significant part was a visit to France, from November 1791 to December 1792, a period of vital importance in European history, embracing as it did the most dramatic moments of the French

Revolution. When in Blois, he came under the influence of a French army officer called Beaupuis, whose humanitarianism called forth all Wordsworth's faith in the cause of the Revolution as the hope of saving mankind from social injustice. In Blois, too, he fell in love with a French girl, Annette Vallon, who bore him a daughter, Caroline, in December 1792.

In that month he was recalled to England and for some years his life was unhappy and unsettled. He was distracted by anxiety about Annette, by the poor reception of his two early poems, *Descriptive Sketches* and *An Evening Walk*, and especially, in February 1793, by the English declaration of war on France, which he regarded as the betrayal of the hopes of oppressed humanity. His mental torment was further increased by the violent turn which the French Revolution had taken and the period was one, for him, of great disillusionment. It may have been this which drove him to seek temporary refuge in the doctrines of the philosopher Godwin, who believed that social injustice could be cured by subordinating the passions to the intellect.

Wordsworth's restoration was brought about by the unexpected legacy of a friend, Raisley Calvert, whose bequest of £900 allowed him to set up house with Dorothy in 1795 at Racedown in Dorset. It was in this year, too, that he first met Samuel Taylor Coleridge, and the care and affection of Dorothy, together with Coleridge's companionship and the intellectual stimulus which it offered, brought about a new peace and happiness. In 1797 he and Dorothy moved to Alfoxden to be nearer to Coleridge, who was living at Nether Stowey, and the fruits of this closer relationship were to be seen in the *Lyrical Ballads* of 1798.

After a visit in 1799 to Germany, where Wordsworth

seems already to have been at work on *The Prelude*, he and Dorothy settled at Dove Cottage, Grasmere. The Lake District was to be their regular home from then on, though in 1808 they moved to Allan Bank and in 1813 to Rydal Mount. In 1802 they visited France, Annette and her daughter coming to Calais to meet them. The reason for this meeting is clear for, on his return, Wordsworth married a childhood friend, Mary Hutchinson, who was to bear him five children.

The years at Dove Cottage saw the production of almost all Wordsworth's best poetry. Most of *The Prelude* was written during this period. Outwardly, it was a period of tranquillity and security. The problem of the inheritance was settled, he found a sympathetic and generous patron in Sir George Beaumont, the sales of his poetry increased and in 1813 he was appointed Distributor of Stamps for the county of Westmorland (not quite the sinecure it is sometimes supposed to be). *The Excursion*, his long philosophical poem, itself only a fragment of a greater and more ambitious undertaking, was published in 1814 and a collected edition of his poems appeared in 1815. But the later years of his life were shadowed by the death at sea in 1805 of his brother John, by the loss of two children, by the gradual disintegration of his friendship with Coleridge, by the illness of Dorothy and by the marriage in 1841 and the death in 1847 of his daughter Dora. From this blow Wordsworth never recovered; he died in 1850 and in this year *The Prelude* was published.

From even this brief recital of facts we can see that two emerge as contributory to Wordsworth's individuality. The first of these is that he was an orphan. Unlike the great masters of the 'long poem' of the two preceding centuries, Milton and Pope, Wordsworth was driven into shaping his own life without the support of a generous and accommodating father or a background of domestic and economic stability. Conscious of some compelling inner power, but without the guidance (or perhaps the restriction) of an older generation, he was, in common with certain other Romantic poets, obliged to travel a lonely road in search of his own individuality. That, at a crucial point in his own career he turned to his sister Dorothy and his friend Coleridge is merely a different aspect of the same truth; by then, the real Wordsworth had been formed. In his personal life, in his politics and in his religion he went his own way. His affair with Annette Vallon was an infraction of the narrowing social code of his time; his sympathies with the French Revolution and his unconventional political views caused the Government, comically, to send a spy to report on the subversive activities he was imagined to be engaged on with Coleridge at Alfoxden; though never anti-Christian, he resisted all the pressures exerted on him by his family to become a clergyman. It is easy to forget all this when the later Wordsworth, who became a respectable married man, who accepted the office of a Government post at the hands of a Tory magnate and who composed a series of Ecclesiastical Sonnets, cast an aura of benign respectability over the younger rebel. But we can see that when the young Wordsworth found his poetic voice it would be his own and not the echo of another man's.

The other important circumstance of his birth is that he was born among the 'states-men' of Cumberland and Westmorland, whose sturdy independence acknowledged few superiors and whose egalitarian society encouraged the democratic belief

That a benignant spirit was abroad
Which might not be withstood, that poverty
Abject as this would in a little time
Be found no more, that we should see . . .

.   .   .   .

. . . the people having a strong hand
In framing their own laws; whence better days
To all mankind.

(*The Prelude*, IX, 519–32)

The hard life of the remote upland valleys forged, too, a strong bond of sympathy for the suffering, the hungry and the needy. In Book IV of *The Prelude*, Wordsworth tells how, one moonlit night, he came unexpectedly upon the figure of one of those common pieces of eighteenth century social jetsam, a disbanded soldier, emaciated and distressed:

. . . I could mark him well,
Myself unseen. He was of stature tall,
A span above man's common measure, tall,
Stiff, lank, and upright; a more meagre man
Was never seen before by night or day.
Long were his arms, pallid his hands; his mouth
Looked ghastly in the moonlight.

(IV, 390–6)

After listening to his story, diffidently, but without patronage and in complete respect for the personal dignity of the older man, Wordsworth guided him towards a neighbouring cottage:

. . . At the door I knocked,
And earnestly to charitable care
Commended him as a poor friendless man,
Belated and by sickness overcome.

This humanitarianism was no literary affectation; Wordsworth gave generously what he could afford to the poor; when challenged with misplaced charity he would reply that one must go on giving and the right recipient would turn up. He saw, in the destitute,

> Souls that appear to have no depth at all
> To careless eyes.

When George and Sarah Green of Blentarn Ghyll, 'the poorest people in the vale', failed to return to their six children after visiting a farm sale in Langdale and were found two days later dead near the foot of a precipice, the whole valley rallied in support. Wordsworth canvassed his friends in a circular letter, raising a third of the sum required for the maintenance of the children but insisting on limiting the fund to £500 lest it should excite 'much envy and unkindly feeling among the poor families of this neighbourhood'. Wordsworth and his sister knew what it was to be orphaned but their understanding of their fellow dalesmen enabled them to act with tact and good sense.[1] When, during Wordsworth's first visit to France, he and Beaupuis came across similar destitution, it was only a realization and confirmation of something he had always known:

> . . . And when we chanced
> One day to meet a hunger-bitten girl,
> Who crept along fitting her languid gait
> Unto a heifer's motion, by a cord
> Tied to her arm, and picking thus from the lane

---

[1] The whole very moving story can be read in De Quincey's *Reminiscences of the Lake Poets*, p. 210 in the Everyman edition.

Its sustenance, while the girl with pallid hands
Was busy knitting in a heartless mood
Of solitude, and at the sight my friend
In agitation said, 'Tis against *that*
That we are fighting,' . .

(IX, 519–528)

The poetry, like Wilfrid Owen's, is in the pity. Like
Owen's, it is also in the poetry; it is one mark of Wordsworth's originality that he was able to make it so.

The same humanitarianism which led Wordsworth to
find his subjects in an unprecedented fashion among the
unromantic beggars, leech-gatherers and shepherds of
the Lake District led him also to seek a new and unromantic
way of describing them. Wordsworth was not the first to
depict rural life in poetry. (In measured couplets, Gold-
smith, in *The Deserted Village*, had quietly celebrated the
golden age of English pastoral life and lamented its
departure, while Crabbe had turned the characteristic
satire of the period to the target of country squalor and
poverty.) But Wordsworth was really the first to do so in
simple and straightforward language and without much
recourse to rhetorical devices. It is, indeed, in his literary
opinions that Wordsworth is at his most original and,
from our point of view, most interesting. His views are
contained and most fully expressed in the Preface to the
second edition (1800) of the *Lyrical Ballads*. The *Lyrical
Ballads* set out to surprise and they succeeded; in form,
subject-matter and language they were different from
anything which had gone before and they form a
watershed in English poetry. They are not, of course, our
primary concern, but what Wordsworth has to say in the
Preface concerns so much of his poetry and touches upon
so many aesthetic questions that any reader of Words-

worth's poetry should peruse it with interest and profit. A good deal of the Preface is concerned with the vexed question of poetic diction—whether the language of poetry is different from the language of prose or from the conversational norm of the period in which it is written. What Wordsworth has to say about this is interesting and important but it is not always borne out by his practice in the poetry which followed the *Lyrical Ballads*. What I wish to draw attention to are those passages which relate to the poet as an artist, to his method of composition and to the subject-matter of his poetry.

He tells us that his principal intention was '. . . to choose incidents and situations from common life, and to relate or describe them, throughout, as far as was possible in a selection of the language really used by men, and at the same time, to throw over them a certain colouring of the imagination, whereby ordinary things should be presented to the mind in an unusual aspect; and further, and above all, to make these incidents and situations interesting by tracing in them, truly though not ostentatiously, the primary laws of our nature: chiefly, as far as regards the manner in which we associate ideas in a state of excitement'. For this reason, 'Humble and rustic life was generally chosen, because, in that condition, the essential passions of the heart find a better soil in which they can attain their maturity' ('*Fair seed-time had my soul . . .*'), and because 'in that condition the passions of men are incorporated with the beautiful and permanent forms of nature' ('*Not with the mean and vulgar works of man,/But with high objects and enduring things*').

Poetry, says Wordsworth, does not necessarily concern itself with the grandiose or spectacular. The human mind 'is capable of being excited without the application of gross and violent stimulants'; he deplores the 'degrading thirst after outrageous stimulation' which has 'driven into neglect' the works of Shakespeare and Milton. Poetry should concern itself with 'the operations of the elements, and the appearances of the visible universe; with storm and sunshine, with the revolutions of the seasons, with cold and heat, with loss of friends and kindred, with injuries and resentments, gratitude and hope, with fear and sorrow', in short ,with 'the inherent and indestructible qualities of the human mind'.

That is to say, the poet is not a man divorced from the realities of living and communion with his fellow men, indulging in 'arbitrary and capricious habits or expression, in order to furnish food for fickle tastes, and fickle appetites'. He is 'a man speaking to men' of his own sensations and objects, which are 'the sensations of other men and the objects which interest them'. But it would be wrong to imagine that Wordsworth considered a poet to be in *no* way different from his fellow-men; he will use their language and share their feelings but with a heightened sensitivity and a more vivid communication; he is 'nothing differing in kind from other men, but only in degree'. The degree to which he is different is that he is 'endowed with more lively sensibility,[1] more enthusiasm and tenderness . . . has a greater knowledge of human nature, and a more comprehensive soul, than are supposed to be common among mankind'. His feelings are powerful and his poetry results from their 'spontaneous overflow; . . . it takes its origin from emotion recollected in tranquillity: the emotion is contemplated till, by a species of reaction,

---

[1] Wordsworth means the ability to receive impressions through the senses.

the tranquillity gradually disappears, and an emotion, kindred to that which was before the object of contemplation, is gradually produced, and does itself actually exist in the mind. In this mood composition generally begins. . . . '

A heightened sensibility and strong feelings are only part of a poet's equipment, however. While it may be true that 'all good poetry is the spontaneous overflow of powerful feelings', it is nevertheless also true that 'Poems to which any value can be attached were never produced on any variety of subjects but by a man who, *being possessed of more than usual organic sensibility, had also thought long and deeply.*' (My italics.) The ideal poet is the one who exhibits the perfect union of thought and feeling.

The foregoing is, of course, only the sketchiest survey of an important literary document which is full of perception and which bristles with thorny artistic problems of every kind. I have dwelt on it to even this inadequate length, however, because I think that it illuminates several aspects of the nature and composition of *The Prelude*. In it we can observe, among other things: the humanitarian basis of much of Wordsworth's poetry; the importance of the heightened sensitivity of an artist speaking to his fellow men of what they know, but dimly realize; the value to Wordsworth of emotion recollected in tranquillity and hence of his dependence on his early experience as the raw material of his long and deep contemplation; the significance of a rural environment as a background to that experience; the transforming power of imagination; the re-creation in the mind of the poet, and hence of the reader, of the emotional force of a deeply-felt experience; the way in which ideas are associated in a state of excitement or heightened awareness; the

B

high seriousness and profound dedication of which he
speaks in Book IV:

> Ah! need I say, dear Friend! that to the brim
> My heart was full; I made no vows, but vows
> Were then made for me;
>
> (IV, 333–5)

and the rooting of that emotion, as always with Wordsworth, in a vividly perceived actual experience, conveyed
with the precision and clarity which is its own best
justification:

> . . . Magnificent
> The morning rose, in memorable pomp,
> Glorious as e'er I had beheld—in front,
> The sea lay laughing at a distance; near,
> The solid mountains shone, bright as the clouds,
> Grain-tinctured, drenched in empyrean light;
> And in the meadows and the lower grounds
> Was all the sweetness of a common dawn—
> Dews, vapours, and the melody of birds,
> And labourers going forth to till the fields.
>
> (IV, 324–33)

A Long Poem

There remain, however, two other general questions
concerning *The Prelude* which we should ask ourselves.
Why is Wordsworth so occupied with himself in relation
to Nature in this 'unprecedented' fashion? Why should
we wish to read so apparently personal a document in which
he talks 'so much about himself'?

The Prelude is the great 'long poem' of the nineteenth
century and it is illuminating to compare it with the impor-

tant 'long poems' of the two preceding centuries. Milton's *Paradise Lost* is the major 'philosophical' poem of the seventeenth century and it is cast in the traditional form of the epic. It is probably fair to say that it is the last real English epic and it is certainly true to say that the choice of its subject gave Milton some trouble. Even by Milton's day, the traditional use of mythology as epic machinery (gods and goddesses who manipulate the action) was becoming difficult. The new scientific movement, challenging as it did the authenticity of all fables and legends, left him only the Bible as a source of material which, as a Christian, he could believe to be true. He tells us that his original intention was to write an Arthuriad,

> . . . to dissect
> With long and tedious havoc fabl'd Knights
> In Battels feigned . . .

but that he changed his mind and decided to celebrate instead 'the Better Fortitude / Of patience and heroic Martyrdom'. Wordsworth would have understood (he knew his Milton well) and in Book I of *The Prelude* he tells us how he, too, dallied with

> . . . some British theme, some old
> Romantic tale by Milton left unsung . . .
>
> · · · · · · · · · · · · ·
>
> Of dire enchantments faced and overcome
> By the strong mind, and tales of warlike feats,
> Where spear encountered spear, and sword with sword
> Fought, as if conscious of the blazonry
> That the shield bore, so glorious was the strife,

(I, 168–79)

but dismissed it in favour of

> . . . some philosophic song
> Of Truth that cherishes our daily life;
> With meditations passionate from deep
> Recesses in man's heart . . .
>
> (I, 229–32)

By Pope's day, in the eighteenth century, there was not available to the poet any longer even the degree of Christian mythology open to Milton. Epic was possible only in translation of the ancients or as mock heroic in *The Dunciad* or *The Rape of the Lock*, where the epic machinery consists of comic sylphs, expressly not to be taken seriously except in a very sophisticated way. If, then, we regard Pope's *Essay on Man* as the long 'philosophic song' of the eighteenth century we can see it as a further de-mythologizing of Milton's theme, the Forbidden Tree replaced by the temptations of the world around us, Adam by the just, moderate man, Eden by an inner contentment. By the time Wordsworth came to write his long philosophic poem there were really only two alternatives available— either the poet had to construct his own mythology and give to it his own significance, or he had to build his poetry out of the interaction of his own personality with the world around him, with no interventions or distractions. Keats chose the first way, Wordsworth the second. The best way of demonstrating the difference is to compare two representative passages. Here is Keats's Moneta, priestess and prophetess, a kind of symbol of knowledge beyond suffering, of a 'wise passiveness':

> . . . Then I saw a wan face,
> Not pin'd by human sorrows, but bright-blanch'd

By an immortal sickness which kills not;
It works a constant change, which happy death
Can put no end to; deathwards progressing
To no death was that visage; it had past
The lily and the snow; and beyond these
I must not think now, though I saw that face—
But for her eyes I should have fled away.

                    (*Fall of Hyperion*, I, 256–65)

She warns him,

> None can usurp this height. . . .
> But those to whom the miseries of the world
> Are misery, and will not let them rest.

When Wordsworth encounters a figure 'with the same *ghastly mildness* in his look', he finds him, typically, in the discharged soldier whom we have met in Book IV of *The Prelude*:

> . . . a more meagre man
> Was never seen before by night or day.
> Long were his arms, pallid his hands, his mouth
> Looked ghastly in the moonlight . . .
>
> .   .   .   .
>
> He all the while was in demeanour calm,
> Concise in answer; solemn and sublime
> He might have seemed, but that in all he said
> There was a strange half-absence, as of one
> Knowing too well the importance of his theme,
> But feeling it no longer.
>
>   (IV, 440–5)

Wordsworth, 'to whom the miseries of the world' were misery,

> . . . earnestly to charitable care
> Commended him as a poor friendless man.

This is not to say that Wordsworth is the better poet or that Keats was not capable of practical generosity, only that the two poets took different paths towards the same truth. It is characteristic and significant that, for Wordsworth, the path was not a metaphorical one; it was the road from Windermere to Hawkshead.

It was a lonely and difficult way. To compose a long poem on Man and Nature, to attempt, without the support of a philosophic system, to revitalize and reanimate what he called 'the universe of death' and to attempt to convert it to one

> . . . which moves with light and life informed,
> Actual, divine and true,
>
> (XIV, 161–2)

placed a heavy burden on the poet's own resources. It had to come, in Coleridge's words, 'From the dread watchtower of man's absolute self'. In Wordsworth's case, what happened was that he built up *from his own experience* (one cannot over-emphasize this) a belief that the mind was capable of interaction with the universe to produce a significant relationship. If we look at the passages of *The Prelude* where Wordsworth recounts incidents which were to him meaningful and important we can see that they are nearly always those in which his mind actively and creatively collaborates with what he is seeing or doing, though at the time he may have been unaware of this:

> . . . An auxiliar light
> *Came from my mind*, which on the setting sun
> Bestowed *new splendour*.
>
> (II, 368–70)

When Coleridge wished to praise Wordsworth's achievement, in a poem composed the night after Wordsworth had read *The Prelude* to him, he chose a similar image:

> When power streamed from thee and thy soul received
> The light reflected as the light bestowed.

The raw material of such experiences lay in the sense impressions which Wordsworth, as a man 'possessed of more than usual organic sensibility', felt so startlingly as 'Gleams like the flashing of a shield' (I, 586). This 'lively sensibility' was available to him in a fresher and more pristine form in the years of his childhood, as, indeed, it is for most men. The story of the slow decay of this organic perception and its gradual replacement by something less acute but, to Wordsworth, more profound is told in *Tintern Abbey* and the *Immortality Ode*, two poems which we shall need to consider in relation to our text; but *The Prelude* itself offers moving testimony to this loss of brightness:

> . . . the hiding-places of man's power
> Open; I would approach them, but they close.
> I see by glimpses now; when age comes on,
> May scarcely see at all.
>
> (XII, 278–82)

For this reason the first two books of *The Prelude* are of particular interest and offer especial delight, for they deal with Wordsworth's early, formative years when his senses were sharp; and they give us an unforgettable re-creation of his childhood involvement in physical activities and the joys and fears which were their consequence. Wordsworth frequently derives from these experiences a theory or philosophy of life; but while it is true that such discussion gives a coherence and form to the whole poem and underlines the importance of the incidents, it is the experiences themselves which interest us, for the vividness with which they are re-enacted carries with it its own guarantee of authenticity.

The first two books of *The Prelude* are studded with such moments—skating, boating, climbing, snaring, riding—and when we read them we can, as we re-live Wordsworth's experiences, understand why he found in them the prime source of his poetic vigour.

It is this which provides us with one answer to our question about the value of reading *The Prelude*—that the sharply-realized *individuality* of the experience justifies itself by its detail, its precision and the power of its re-telling. It is not likely, unless we elected to do so, that we should be convinced by Wordsworth's theorizing if it took place in an artistic vacuum; it is doubtful if psychology and natural science between them would allow us to accept this particular formulation of his beliefs, which are either naïve or mystical, according to how you look at them. What we *can* be sure of, what we *can* testify to, are the *truth* of the experiences themselves, because they are observed so closely and presented so clearly, and the *significance* of those experiences, because they were understood by Wordsworth as valuable to himself and are communicated as such to his readers. The experiences are, to use a loose descriptive term, 'psychologically' true, as stages in the 'growth of a poet's mind'.

But the *individuality* of this experience, however

accurately depicted, is only one answer to the value of *The Prelude*. The other lies in its *typicality*. This is not so simple as saying either that all men have had the same experiences as Wordsworth or that only those who have can read his poetry, but only that generations of readers have recognized in it images which Dr. Johnson described as finding 'a mirrour in every mind' and passages which, in Keats's words, 'strike the reader as a wording of his own highest thoughts and appear almost a Remembrance'. What distinguishes the poet, said Wordsworth, is 'a greater promptness to think and feel without immediate external excitement, and a greater power in expressing such thoughts and feelings'. But these thoughts and feelings are not remote from those of common humanity, though the incidents which give rise to them may be personal; they are 'the general passions and thoughts and feelings of men'. So, when Coleridge was thinking of publishing his lines to Wordsworth on the composition of *The Prelude*, he hesitated. 'It is for the biographer', he said, 'not the poet, to give the accidents of individual life. Whatever is not *representative*, *generic*, may indeed be poetically expressed, but it is not poetry.' It is because Wordsworth believed that his poetry *was* 'representative' and 'generic' that he relied implicitly on his personal vision and the accidents of his individual life as the source of his poetic power. It is through this paradox that the egotistical became sublime.

Some Questions:

1. 'A selection of the language really used by men.' How far is this the basis of poetry in general or of Wordsworth's poetry in particular?

2. Do you think that subjects drawn from everyday life are inherently more suitable material for poetry than others?

3. How far is your appreciation of a writer's work affected by a knowledge of his biography?

4. Can literature which is largely autobiographical make a contribution to the enlargement of human experience?

5. The 'long poem' is no longer fashionable. Can you think of reasons for its decline? What attempts have been made to replace it? You might consider *The Waste Land*, *Four Quartets* and *The Age of Anxiety*.

6. Discuss the ways in which a writer may use a 'myth', even one in which he does not literally believe, as the basis of a work of imagination.

7. How far is the enjoyment of Wordsworth's poetry attributable to enthusiasm for his characteristic subject-matter?

Suggested reading:

Ed. Colette Clarke: *Home at Grasmere* (Penguin Books).
De Quincey: *Reminiscences of the Lake Poets*.
Hazlitt: *My First Acquaintance with Poets*.
Wordsworth: *The Old Cumberland Beggar* and *Michael*.
Keats: *Hyperion*.

'MORE THAN HISTORIC'

1. *The Prelude*

The Prelude is not the title by which Wordsworth would have recognized his long poem. He called it always the 'poem on his own early life' or the 'poem to Coleridge'. The title was given to it by Mary Wordsworth when it was prepared for publication in 1850 after Wordsworth's death. Wordsworth had never intended that it should be published in his lifetime; he may, at one stage, have intended that it should not be published at all. It is the version of 1850 which is most frequently reprinted and read but it is important to realize that by 1805 an earlier version of the poem had been completed. During the intervening period, the first version underwent considerable revision, notably in the years 1828, 1832 and 1839, as Wordsworth's opinions and literary habits changed, so that what we have in the final version is a kind of palimpsest of Wordsworth's changing attitudes, rather as if we were viewing his formative years through the telescopic lens of his maturity. It is, therefore, a very complex poem and it is perhaps a mistake to look for complete consistency and accuracy throughout its fourteen books. The version of 1805 has been printed in a handy format[1] and it is highly thought of by many critics for the simplicity and freshness of its style. Wordsworth's revisions (which make interesting material for the discussion of the style of the 1850

---

[1] *The Prelude.* Text of 1805, ed. de Selincourt. Revised by Helen Darbishire, O.U.P., 1964.

27

text) take briefly the following main forms: the original straightforward language is often replaced by more elevated, 'literary' expression; some ambiguities (not all) are removed; the tone becomes less private after Wordsworth's partial estrangement from Coleridge and there is a tendency for Wordsworth to theorize about his experiences and to modify some of his ideas to accord with his later Christian orthodoxy.

The poem seems to have been begun in tentative fashion in Germany in 1798–99 (perhaps even earlier). Some fragments—'There was a boy . . .' (Book V) and the skating episode—were published in 1800 and 1809 respectively, the latter under the significant title: 'Influence of Natural objects in calling forth and strengthening the imagination in Boyhood and early Youth.' Books I and II were completed by 1800 and the poem was then laid aside for two or three years. This is of interest because it allows us to regard the first two books as a unit without doing violence to Wordsworth's design for the whole work.

The best account of the origin of *The Prelude* is given by Wordsworth himself, in the Preface to *The Excursion* (1814):

'Several years ago, when the Author retired to his native mountains, with the hope of being able to construct a literary work that might live, it was a reasonable thing that he should take a review of his own mind, and examine how far Nature and Education had qualified him for such employment. As subsidiary to this preparation, he undertook to record, in verse, the origin and progress of his own powers, as far as he was acquainted with them. . . . The preparatory poem is biographical, and conducts the history of the Author's mind to the point when he was emboldened to hope that his faculties were sufficiently matured for entering upon the arduous labour which he had proposed to himself.'

Wordsworth is telling us the most important thing about *The Prelude*—that it is a voyage of exploration; not a diary, not a source of information, but a self-examination. It is because it has this exploratory quality that it is continually created afresh in the minds of its readers. The poem grew in scope and length during its composition. A passage deleted (luckily) from the final version of Book V tells us:

> . . . as this work was taking in my thoughts
> Proportions that seemed larger than had first
> Been meditated, I was indisposed
> To any further progress at a time
> When these acknowledgements were left unpaid.

Though Wordsworth calls his poem 'biographical', it is never that in a straightforward chronological way. Events do not always follow each other in the order in which they happened and the poem is shaped by a kind of internal logic of the growth of the poet's mind rather than by the sequence of external events. In this fashion, one of the most moving passages in *The Prelude*—his account of how he waited impatiently for the horses which were to take him home for the Christmas holidays during which his father died and the family was orphaned—occurs not in Books I or II where we might expect it, but in Book XII, because it illustrates one of the 'spots of time' with which our life is illuminated:

> And, afterwards, the wind and sleety rain,
> And all the business of the elements,
> The single sheep, and the one blasted tree,

And the bleak music from that old stone wall,
The noise of wood and water, and the mist
That on the line of those two roads
Advanced in such indisputable shapes;
All these were kindred spectacles and sounds
To which I oft repaired, and thence would drink,
As at a fountain . . .

(XII, 317-26)

and it occurs there, not because it has been saved up as a useful illustration but because it springs naturally from the 'visionary dreariness' which Wordsworth has just been re-living in the previous passage.

There are other examples: the actual biographical material does not begin until line 269 of Book I; Book VIII is called 'Retrospect' and consists of a recapitulation of events and Book IX begins with a long simile to explain this diversion from the main theme:

Even as a river,—partly (it might seem)
Yielding to old remembrances, and swayed
In part by fear to shape a way direct,
That would engulph him soon in the ravenous sea—
Turns, and will measure back his course, far back,
Seeking the very regions which he crossed
In his first outset; so have we, my Friend!
Turned and returned with intricate delay.

(IX, 1-9)

There is, of course, good reason for Wordsworth's arrangement of his material; just as he preferred not to publish his poems in chronological order lest it should seem that their importance lay in their account of the order of his feelings rather than in their inherent significance, so, in *The Prelude*, he similarly avoids the simply chronological arrangement of material in favour of one which would emphasize the essential importance of certain experiences and states of mind. I think it is not possible to do justice to *The Prelude* unless we see that it is in this respect a novel and original undertaking in its examination and linking of the factors, both important and trivial, which go to make up a complex human personality. So Wordsworth's story is built up not only out of obviously important personal or historical events like his Cambridge education or the French Revolution but also out of apparently trivial ones like hearing a wren sing in a deserted chapel or the dry wind blowing round the naked crags. In his realization of the importance of the smallest event in the development of the personality Wordsworth is curiously modern. He knew the difficulties:

> Hard task, vain hope, to analyse the mind,
> If each most obvious and particular thought,
> Not in a mystical and idle sense,
> But in the words of Reason deeply weighed,
> Hath no beginning.
> (II, 227-31)

and he realized that readers less perceptive than he would find his approach bewildering:

> The matter that detains us now may seem,
> To many, neither dignified enough
> Nor arduous, yet will not be scorned by them,
> Who, looking inward, have observed the ties
> That bind the perishable hours of life
> Each to the other, and the curious props

By which the world of memory and thought
Exists and is sustained.

                                    (VII, 458–465)

There are two important passages in Book I where
Wordsworth attempts to account for his awareness of
impressions which, though they may be only partially
recognized and understood at the time, leave a permanent
imprint on the mind:

> . . . the earth
> And common face of Nature spake to me
> Rememberable things; sometimes, 'tis true,
> By chance collisions and quaint accidents
> (Like those ill-sorted unions, work supposed
> Of evil-minded fairies), yet not vain
> Nor profitless, if haply they impressed
> Collateral objects and appearances,
> Albeit lifeless then, and doomed to sleep
> Until maturer seasons called them forth
> To impregnate and to elevate the mind.
>
>   (I, 586–96)

In the second passage he is accounting for the way in
which experiences which are frightening or unpleasant in
themselves can nevertheless have ultimately a beneficial
effect on the growth of personality:

> Dust as we are, the immortal spirit grows
> Like harmony in music; there is a dark
> Inscrutible workmanship that reconciles
> Discordant elements, makes them cling together
> In one society. How strange that all
> The terrors, pains and early miseries,
> Regrets, vexations, lassitudes interfused

Within my mind, should e'er have borne a part,
And that a needful part, in making up
The calm existence that is mine when I
Am worthy of myself!

(I, 340–50)

The two passages together form an extended version of what Wordsworth means when he says, at the beginning of the account of his childhood, in lines which are the key to the first two books of *The Prelude*:

Fair seed-time had my soul, and I grew up
Fostered alike by beauty and by fear.

(I, 301–2)

Wordsworth's especial contribution in *The Prelude* to our understanding of the ways in which human character is developed is not to be found simply in passages like these where he discusses his ideas. It is to be found rather in the way in which the sharp detail and vivid re-creation of the sensations of childhood exhilaration, of the movement of the sky and the turning world, of the sound of a lonely flute or a boy calling to the owls by a glimmering lake, of

. . . notes that are
The ghostly language of the ancient earth,

(II, 308–9)

enable the reader to participate in those experiences so that they become meaningful to him and he can transcend the barrier of language to hear, with the poet,

. . . the mind's
Internal echo of the imperfect sound.

(I, 54–5)

c

To Coleridge, the poem was 'More than historic'; it was 'that Prophetic lay'.

Another reason why many readers find in *The Prelude* an endorsement of their own experience is that the act of composition was for Wordsworth himself a therapeutic one. There are indications in the first books that he sometimes felt frustrated and anxious lest Coleridge's faith in his genius might not be justified:

> Far better never to have heard the name
> Of zeal and just ambition, than to live
> Baffled and plagued by a mind that every hour
> Turns recreant to her task; takes heart again,
> Then feels immediately some hollow thought
> Hang like an interdict upon her hopes.
>
> (I, 255–60)

It seemed to him that he might be

> Unprofitably travelling towards the grave,
> Like a false steward who hath much received
> And renders nothing back.

At the end of Book I, his spirits are high:

> One end at least hath been attained; my mind
> Hath been revived. . . .

He is a different man; and it is the sense of sharing the hesitant, haphazard and sometimes uneven progress of Wordsworth's mind towards this condition which helps to convince the reader of the truth of the experience and makes him, too, partly a different person.

2. Books I and II: 'The Child is Father of the Man.'

Bearing in mind, then, that we would not expect to find in Books I and II of *The Prelude* a straightforward autobiography, let us examine the design of the two books, first of all placing them in the general context of the complete poem.

Books I and II are concerned mainly with Wordsworth's childhood and boyhood experiences amid the natural surroundings of the Lake District; Book III enlarges his experience of men and letters during his 'submissive idleness' at Cambridge, 'ill-tutored for captivity' and Book IV gives an account of the summer vacation when he returned to his 'native hills'. The four books may be seen as the first movement of the poem, culminating in the poet's dedication in Book IV:

> . . . I made no vows but vows
> Were then made for me. . . .

After this first movement, the narrative is suspended as Wordsworth reviews, in Book V, his early debt to books and reading. Books VI and VII tell of his walking holiday in the Alps and his subsequent residence in London and there is a second pause in Book VIII as Wordsworth retrospectively surveys his childhood and growing maturity. The title of this Book: 'Love of Nature Leading to Love of Man', indicates its centrality and acts almost like an emblem of the whole poem. Books IX and X record the progress of Wordsworth's hopes for humanity in the French Revolution and reach a climax in the betrayal of those hopes and Wordsworth's consequent depression and disillusionment. The last movement of the poem, Books XI to XIV, tells of the gradual restoration of his faith in humanity through the agency of Dorothy, Coleridge and 'Love of Nature' and of the recovery and consecration of his vocation as a poet.

But Books I and II are the most important, as they are

the most enjoyable. In them Wordsworth traces the childhood experiences which he valued so highly as the means by which the life of the senses entered and informed the life of the spirit. They record his attempts to

> . . . rescue from decay the old
> By timely interference,

to snatch from oblivion the precious moments which were the fountain-light of his poetic powers.

Book I

The poem opens with a curiously Wordsworthian version of the traditional call for inspiration at the beginning of a long poem; it is not the breath of the muses or of Milton's 'warning voice' which is to be breathed into him but a literal breeze, bringing joy from the 'green fields' and the 'azure sky', like 'the sweet breath of heaven'. While it fans his cheek, Wordsworth finds that, 'escaped from the vast city', he can 'breathe again', for he finds within himself 'a correspondent breeze'. In this celebration of a sense of release (in this case, from confinement in the city) and the breaking-up of 'a long-continued frost', the lines are reminiscent of the openings of two other famous poems far apart in time and nature, poems as disparate as *The Canterbury Tales* and *The Waste Land*.

Wordsworth tells us that he hopes to begin his poetic work in 'active days urged on by flying hours'. It is not habitual for him to write so spontaneously; he is not 'used to make/A present joy the matter of a song' but his powerful feelings overflow and he begins to compose aloud (this was his usual practice) encouraged by the 'imperfect' sound of his poetry but more by the ideal echo of it heard inside himself and by the awareness that

> . . . a higher power
> Than Fancy gave assurance of some work
> Of glory there forthwith to be begun.

Arrived at his destination (it would seem to be Racedown) he determines to brace himself for the task either by reading up new material or by thinking about and re-capturing his past experience as a source of inspiration:

> . . . either to lay up
> New stores, or rescue from decay the old
> By timely interference.

But a poetic sensibility is not an easy one to control, nor will it always obey the call to action; his 'Unmanageable thoughts' frustrate his attempts to write. To prepare himself, Wordsworth first makes a 'rigorous inquisition' of his own resources. The report, he says, is encouraging. He seems to have the necessary equipment for the task— the 'vital soul' which enables the poet to carry his truth alive into the heart by passion; and 'general truths' in the form of axioms of philosophy 'proved upon our pulses' by experience (Keats) which give coherence and support to his random impressions, those 'external things' with which his mind is stored. What he lacks is a subject; like Milton before him, he considers tales of chivalry or epics which celebrate (characteristically for Wordsworth) some spirited defence of liberty, only to reject them in favour of 'some philosophic song/Of Truth that cherishes our daily life'. But he recoils from this 'awful burthen' in the hope that 'mellower years will bring a riper mind'. Wordsworth is honest enough to record that this was a form of self-deception:

> Humility and modest awe themselves
> Betray me, serving often for a cloak
> To a more subtle selfishness,

and he resigns himself to 'vacant musing' and 'deliberate holiday'. This in turn produces a feeling of frustration and lassitude at his failure to pursue 'zeal and just ambition'. He feels he can return nothing of what life has given him. At this point, to lift himself out of his general depression, he asks what it is that life *has* offered him and he finds that from his earliest childhood the influence of his environment has informed his character, giving him

> A foretaste, a dim earnest, of the calm
> That Nature breathes among the hills and groves.

The River Derwent, 'fairest of all rivers', shared the process of his upbringing with his nurse, sending 'a voice / That flowed along my dreams'.

It may be appropriate here, before we come to Wordsworth's other childhood recollections, to draw attention to the way in which Wordsworth's meaning depends absolutely on the actual words he uses in his descriptive evocations. Indeed, stripped of their language and the feeling of actuality produced by the apparently inconsequential details which Wordsworth records, many of his ideas can be made to appear irrational. But Wordsworth is writing about a connection of various strands of experience which is not in itself a logical connection and he presents his ideas not in isolation but surrounded by the contributory circumstances—the bright blue river, the

yellow ragwort, the bronzed woods, distant Skiddaw—
which give them their ring of truth.

From these early recollections Wordsworth is led into
writing an account of his boyhood life by way of the
important lines which neatly epitomize the first two books:

> Fair seed-time had my soul, and I grew up
> Fostered alike *by beauty and by fear.*

These two emotions and the incidents which provoked
them were the controlling factors in his development and
the events which he now proceeds to relate offer evidence
of one, or other, or both. Snaring woodcocks gives the
exhilaration of the frosty wind and the beauty of the last
autumnal crocus, but also, in its association with a
feeling of guilt at having taken another boy's catch, the
fear of 'Low breathings' and 'steps/Almost as silent as
the turf they trod'; climbing after a raven's nest supplies
the excitement of the moving clouds but also the formative
discipline of danger on the 'perilous ridge'. We cannot,
says Wordsworth, ever fully understand the 'Inscrutable
workmanship' that links these experiences and gives them
a coherent meaning. Often the emotion will be powerful,
if Nature makes one of her 'severer interventions', as
when the boy stole a boat one summer evening in an act
of 'troubled pleasure'. Beauty there certainly was, in the
'Small circles glittering idly in the moon' but it was also
accompanied by guilt and fear in his vision of the towering
peak and the impression it gave him of 'unknown modes of
being'.

In the lines which follow, Wordsworth argues that
images such as these, which are the source of great
emotion, pass from the organic senses of ear and eye into
a perpetual existence in the mind where, in the association

of these emotions with the awful and majestic, rather than with the base and sordid, they sanctify by their discipline,

> Both pain and fear, until we recognise
> A grandeur in the beatings of the heart.

Sometimes, as in the skating episode which follows and which we shall examine in detail later, the sensation may be the almost mystical one of the earth's rolling with visible motion. Simple pleasures like nutting, fishing or kite-flying all exert their influence. The 'milk-white clusters' of the hazel-nuts are the tokens of desire, the unsuccessful rod and line 'true symbol of hope's foolishness', the paper kite, 'suddenly/Dashed headlong', the emblem of elation and disappointment; all are anticipations of experience in the larger world and help to prepare for that experience.

In addition to this growing awareness of Nature resulting from external influences and impressions ('extrinsic passion') he also feels *within himself* a sense of union with Nature which he attributes to our 'first-born affinities' (an idea which he develops at length in lines 232–64 of Book II and returns to in the *Immortality Ode*). Sometimes, indeed, his 'intercourse with beauty' has been unconscious and on a purely physical level, a simple delight in the curling mist or the shining moon-lit water; but at other times it has produced a mystical sensation, 'Gleams like the flashing of a shield.' No one, says Wordsworth, knows how these things come to be associated but his

Even indoors, in home amusements 'too humble to be named in verse', he was always aware of the power of Nature's 'keen and silent tooth' and of the protracted sound of 'Esthwaite's splitting fields of ice'.

experience tells him that 'By the impressive discipline of fear,/By pleasure and repeated happiness' these scenes are bound to our personalities by invisible and indissoluble links. For this reason, he will have recourse to the earliest springs of his childhood experience, 'that I might fetch/Invigorating thoughts from former years'. The act of doing so has already proved beneficial; his mind has been revived and the subject of his poem is now clear to him. In the certain knowledge that his own experience is his best guide, he now recognizes that the road lies plain before him and that Coleridge will be there to welcome him at the end of the journey.

Book II

Wordsworth again remembers the boisterous pleasures of his youth when his passion for Nature was in its infancy and was fed, unsolicited, by a careless 'round of tumult' that lasted well into the evening and left him and his comrades healthily exhausted. He wishes that he could recover these high spirits in the cause of duty and truth and the contemplation of them produces something like a double-vision:

> . . . musing on them do I seem
> Two consciousnesses, conscious of myself
> And of some other Being.

It is as if he had double-exposed a film of the same scene, once with the rude mass of native rock at the centre of the market-place and again, much later, with the new Assembly Rooms superimposed upon the original.

In time, he sought less boisterous enjoyments—boat-racing on Windermere where, under the auspices of

Nature, the emotions of jealousy and disappointment had no meaning and those of pride and ambition were exercised in an environment which gave them free play without harmful effects:

> . . . thus was gradually produced
> A quiet independence of the heart.

Sometimes, when they had a little money in their pockets after the holidays, they would hire horses from the inn-keeper (without always telling him how far they intended to go) and ride to Furness Abbey where once he enjoyed a moment of stillness that he wished could last for ever while a single wren 'sang so sweetly in the nave'. At other times they would ride to the sea or play bowls on the green of the 'White Lion' at Bowness. Again Wordsworth records the sensation of sudden stillness after feverish activity, the feeling which he caught memorably in the Westminster Bridge sonnet:

> N'er saw I, never felt, a calm so deep!

and which seems to be a common pattern in his experience. On this occasion it was produced by one of his comrades whom they had left playing his flute upon a rock; the calm of the scene sank down into Wordsworth's heart and held him like a dream.

Then, gradually a change came over his appreciation of Nature; he began to seek her 'For her own sake.' But the change was subtle and Wordsworth asks how it is possible to determine with any accuracy the precise moment at which such and such a cause begins to affect the development of the intellect. What science is there which can measure this 'by geometric rules'? He appeals to Coleridge, as a man who has gone into these things more fully, to confirm that such measurements, such boundaries and distinctions, are *made* by man, not *discovered* by him; that Science, however necessary it may be, is only a substitute for insight, and that any attempt to produce a schematic analysis of the mind will founder, if the origins of our ideas cannot be traced to a particular and well-defined source. Even in the 'infant Babe' some 'first affections' may be observed. The child does not perceive things merely as objects; they are already coloured for him by 'the feelings of his Mother's eye'. A flower is not just a flower but one already made beautiful by his mother's attitude of love; a hurt creature engages his sympathy because of an 'inward tenderness' caught from his mother. The universe into which he is born is not neutral but 'active' and in time he learns to work 'in alliance' with it, not merely *receiving* impressions but reacting positively to them to make a meaningful experience. In this, says Wordsworth, lies the origin of the poetic spirit; in most people, this faculty is 'abated or suppressed' by the sheer atrophying process of living; in others, like himself, it continues to the end 'through every change of growth and decay'. This is the theme of the great *Immortality Ode*.

Next follows a passage in whose 'broken windings' he tries to trace the gradual growth of his independent relationship with Nature when once the support of these natural affections had been removed. This closer communion, in which every advance in knowledge meant greater delight, brought with it increased insight and a 'Sublimer joy' in moments of 'shadowy exultation', which, because their 'visionary power' suggests to the soul a kind of sublime experience, also encourage that soul to persevere in the continual search of this sublimity. Sometimes this new-found relationship with Nature would bring, on his early walks round the lake, the opposite feeling of a 'holy calm', in the ecstasy of which he became almost unaware of things as having an independent existence, so much did they seem a part of himself. For a 'natural' mystic like Wordsworth, the evocation of such visions depended on the stimulus presented by his senses rather than merely on a process of contemplation. For this reason, for Wordsworth, neither Nature, nor the vision, was simply illusory. Although it was necessary to transcend the senses in order to perceive the 'reality' behind Nature, Nature itself was the medium through which the 'reality' was exhibited, just as the organic senses were the medium through which the experience was transmitted to the 'real' Wordsworth. This is, of course, an attempt to explain in rational terms an experience which is beyond the scope of reason to analyse; yet we should notice again that, just as the visionary moments depend upon the senses for their evocation, so this difficult and quasi-mystical notion is not presented in isolation but is prepared for by the vivid clarity of the scene which precedes it.

From a succession of such moments he learned to avoid the merely passive admiration of Nature and to replace it by an exercise of the modifying power of his own mind so that this creative act of transformation gave him a highly personal vision:

> . . . An auxiliar light
> Came from my mind, which on the setting sun
> Bestowed new splendour.

In this way he learned also to connect different varieties of experience which, 'to passive minds', remain disjointed, so that, by the time he was seventeen, he had reached a condition of supreme happiness in the awareness of the unity of all created life, animated by

> . . . the sentiment of Being spread
> O'er all that moves and all that seemeth still.

In the final section, Wordsworth expresses his gratitude to the forces of Nature for making him what he is. If, in times when the failure of the French Revolution is causing even good men to abandon their hope for the betterment of the human race, he himself still retains his faith in human nature, it is owing to these forces: 'the gift is yours'. The Book ends with a greeting to Coleridge in lines which, in their echo of the opening of Book I, bring our text round full circle:

> . . . Thou, my Friend! wert reared
> In the great city, 'mid far other scenes;
> But we, by different roads, at length have gained
> The self-same bourne.

Some questions:

1. What advantages are there for Wordsworth in his non-chronological scheme?

2. 'The child is father of the man', wrote Wordsworth in another poem. What did he mean by this? How is it demonstrated in *The Prelude*, Books I and II?

3. 'The success of Wordsworth's poetry depends on his ability to recreate in the mind of the reader an emotion comparable with that which he himself experienced.' Discuss.

4. 'Wordsworth's mystical experiences can be appreciated

only in so far as an aesthetic equivalent for them is found objectively in the medium of his poetry'. Discuss.

Suggested reading:

The Journal of Dorothy Wordsworth.
Wordsworth: *The Prelude*, Books IV and VI.

SOME THEMES

We must now try to draw together some recurring themes which are scattered throughout the first two books of *The Prelude*.

1. *Childhood and Maturity*.

Much of Wordsworth's poetry is concerned, like Milton's, with paradise lost and regained. When Adam loses the sensuous delights of Eden he is told by the archangel Michael that he must look for 'A Paradise within'; the story of this loss and hard-won recovery is told in a different way by Wordsworth. The first two books of *The Prelude* celebrate mainly the earlier stages of this development, the joys and fears which, like Adam's, are not lost so much as transformed into a new kind of experience. The whole story, of the awareness of loss and the feeling of compensation for that loss in the greater insight of maturity, is told in two other poems. They are, to give them their full titles: *Lines Composed a Few Miles above Tintern Abbey, on Revisiting the Banks of the Wye During a Tour (1798)* and *Ode: Intimations of Immortality from Recollections of Early Childhood* (pub. 1807). In each the emphasis is slightly different; perhaps *Tintern Abbey* has more to offer of recovery and the *Immortality Ode* more to say about loss, but that is for the reader to judge. The common ground may be seen if we place together a passage from each poem, together with one from *The Prelude*:

a. . . . that time is past,
   And all its aching joys are now no more,
   And all its dizzy raptures. Not for this
   Faint I, nor mourn nor murmur; *other gifts*
   Have followed; for such loss, I would believe,
   Abundant recompense.
                          (*Tintern Abbey,* 83–8)

b. *Though nothing can bring back the hour*
   Of splendour in the grass, of glory in the flower;
         We will grieve not, *rather find*
         Strength in what remains behind;
         In the primal sympathy
         Which having been must ever be;
         In the soothing thoughts that spring
         Out of human suffering;
         In the faith that looks through death,
   In years that bring the philosophic mind.
                          (*Immortality Ode,* 181–90)

c. Oh! mystery of man, from what a depth
   Proceed thy honours. I am lost, *but see*
   In simple childhood something of the base
   On which thy greatness stands; but this I feel,
   That from thyself it comes, that thou must give
   Else never can receive. The days gone by
   Return upon me almost from the dawn
   Of life: the hiding-places of man's power
   Open; I would approach them, but they close.
   I see by glimpses now; when age comes on
   May scarcely see at all.
                          (*The Prelude,* XII, 272–82)

Tintern Abbey

This very beautiful short poem appeared first at the end
of the Lyrical Ballads but, in its blank verse form and its
subjective view of nature, it is closer in style and mood to
The Prelude. Its interest for us here lies in the fact that it
presents powerfully, but in miniature, the changing
pattern of Wordsworth's relationship with Nature and
it illustrates a perception which is central to all Wordsworth's thought: that the nature of the universe changes
with the changing capacity of the beholder to assimilate it.
Wordsworth is revisiting Tintern Abbey, which he has
last seen five years previously. The intervening period has
been one of doubt, stress and disillusionment and, as he
again looks over the landscape with that earlier scene still
in mind, he contemplates what he has gained and lost
in the years which lie between. The poem presents this
double vision dramatically at its close by linking the
younger Wordsworth with his sister Dorothy, who is
present on this second occasion almost as an image of his
former self.

As in those episodes in *The Prelude* where Wordsworth
recounts some quasi-mystical experience, the setting of the
poem is important, for it not only establishes the emotional
tone but also gives, by its accurate perception of the scene,
its guarantee of the authenticity of the experience. The
setting is, as often, one of great natural beauty and
quietness—the only sound is the 'soft inland murmur' of
the Wye; the smoke wreathes its way 'in silence, from
among the trees'. It is, of course, the same landscape as
he had viewed previously: 'Once again I see/These
hedgerows'; it is Wordsworth who has changed. As if to
mark this change, the landscape reflects, in its 'unripe

D

fruits' and 'little lines/Of sportive wood run wild', the early exuberance of Wordsworth's youthful reaction to Nature, and, in the 'steep and lofty cliffs' which impress 'thoughts of more deep seclusion', his more sober appreciation of its powers. The wholeness of the scene, in which the landscape, 'clad in *one* green hue', is connected 'with the quiet of the sky', is an emblem of the unity of creation, of the 'presence' which, as Wordsworth learned from experiences such as these, 'rolls through all things'.

Whatever the intervening years have brought, of one thing Wordsworth is certain—that the 'beauteous forms' of his first glimpse of the Wye valley have stayed with him:

> . . . oft, in lonely rooms and 'mid the din
> Of towns and cities, I have owed to them,
> In hours of weariness, sensations sweet . . .

The pastoral scene and its accompanying emotions, when recollected in retrospect, pass into the mind with 'tranquil restoration'. They flash upon the 'inward eye' of memory whose restorative power leads to that 'serene and blessed mood' in which all the doubts and uncertainties of living are resolved. It is because Wordsworth recognizes the power of such reflection to assuage in himself, by informing his mind with 'quietness and beauty', the bitterness evoked by 'Rash judgments', 'the sneers of selfish men' and 'greetings where no kindness is', that he is able to enlarge this perception to include the whole 'dreary intercourse of daily life'. He does not lose his awareness of human suffering; it still has power to 'chasten and subdue'. But his knowledge that the troubles and frustrations of his own life can be held in perspective by the restorative power of memory enables him to see this operating on a cosmic scale too, in

> . . . the mystery,
> In which the heavy and the weary weight
> Of all this unintelligible world
> Is lightened.

It is, as in *The Prelude*, a necessary part of this experience that the physical senses should be suspended, that we should be 'laid asleep/In body and become *a living soul*', so that we may 'see into the life of things', a condition which is the final reward of careful observation and deep reflection.

Because of this, Wordsworth comes also to believe that, as he again stands by the banks of the Wye,

> . . . in this moment there is life and food
> For future years.

This leads him to review the changes which have come about in his attitude to Nature. He distinguishes three major phases—a condition of sheer physical exuberance, 'when like a roe/I bounded o'er the mountains'; then a more mystical relationship:

> . . . I cannot paint
> What then I was. The sounding cataract
> Haunted me like a passion;

and then, finally, a mature and thoughtful sobriety, based on his growing awareness of human suffering and mortality. This has taught him to look on Nature 'not as in the hour/Of thoughtless youth' but as if the whole bitter-sweetness of life itself made, by a kind of harmony and counterpoint of its complex and interlocking parts, 'The still, sad music of humanity.'

This feeling of the essential harmony of disparate

human experiences leads him to an awareness of the unity of all creation:

> . . . a sense sublime
> Of something, far more deeply interfused
> Whose dwelling is the light of setting suns,
> And the round ocean and the living air,
> And the blue sky and in the mind of man.

It is an awareness which is based upon the *interaction* of mind and matter:

> . . . of all the mighty world
> Of eye and ear—*both what they half create,*
> *And what perceive,*

for the landscape exists partly in the eye of the beholder, since he brings to it a changing and developing capacity to interpret what he sees.

Though this sense of unity is far from his later orthodoxy, Wordsworth clearly feels that Nature has revealed itself to him as the visible manifestation of deity; as yet, however, he expresses no feeling of need for the central mysteries of the Christian faith; the exaltation of his soul springs from 'natural' impulses.

The poem goes beyond this to show how the memory of natural beauty may contribute to human morality as exhibited in the actions of the good man:

> His little, nameless, unremembered acts
> Of kindness and of love,

and ends as Wordsworth sees, in his sister Dorothy, his earlier self. He hopes that for her, too, 'wild ecstasies shall be matured/Into a sober pleasure'. Yet Dorothy is not merely a companion or a passive observer of the 'green pastoral landscape'. She is herself a part of Wordsworth's 'sober pleasure' in the 'steep woods and lofty cliffs', which are the more precious to him for her sake.

The Immortality Ode

The first stanzas of this poem celebrate, though in a more complicated lyrical form, the initial stages of the relationship with Nature which Wordsworth records in *Tintern Abbey*—the sheer physical delight in external beauty and the 'visionary gleam' which it produced:

> There was a time when meadow, grove, and stream,
>   The earth and every common sight
>   To me did seem
>   Apparelled in celestial light,
> The glory and the freshness of a dream.

But across these lines fall the flat monosyllables of:

The things which I have seen I now can see no more.

Wordsworth tries to revive his earlier enthusiasm but his difficulty is revealed in the slightly strained exuberance of the third and fourth stanzas. When the strong shadow of empty reality falls again over the poem at the end of Stanza IV:

> But there's a Tree, of many, one,
> A single Field which I have looked upon,
> Both of them speak of something that is gone:
>   The pansy at my feet
>   Doth the same tale repeat:
> Whither is fled the visionary gleam?
> Where is it now, the glory and the dream?'

we think we know what the poem is to be about—the loss
of 'a splendour in the objects of sense'; it confirms his
need to recapture, in *The Prelude,* those fleeting sources of
inspiration. At this point Wordsworth put the poem
down. When he took it up again, some two years later, he
attempted an answer to the closing questions.

He found it in the notion of a heavenly pre-existence,
the splendour of which fades 'into the light of common
day'. We do not need to acknowledge a literal belief in
this idea in order to enjoy the poem. Wordsworth himself
tells us, 'I took hold of the notion of pre-existence as
having sufficient foundation in humanity for encouraging
me to make for my purpose the best use I could of it as
a Poet', and modern psychology would allow us to accept
the expulsion from the womb as a type of the same
experience (to each generation its own myths!).

Our interest, as far as *The Prelude* is concerned, lies in
two other aspects of the poem. The first of these is his
idea of the 'first affections' of the child:

> Those shadowy recollections
> Which, be they what they may,
> Are yet the fountain-light of all our day
> Are yet a master-light of all our seeing.

It is from these affections, learned at the mother's knee,
that the mature adult draws the origin of his moral being:

> Is there a flower, to which he points with hand
> Too weak to gather it, *already love*
> *Drawn from love's purest earthly fount for him*
> *Hath beautified that flower.*
>
> (*The Prelude,* II, 245–8)

They are the

> . . . first-born affinities *that fit*
> *Our new existence to existing things,*
> And, in the dawn of being, constitute
> *The bond of union* between life and joy."
> (*The Prelude*, I, 555–8)

The second theme is that which confirms the experience of *Tintern Abbey* and warns us not to regard the real subject of the Ode as simply the loss of poetic power but rather as the compensating discovery of a new and soberer power, springing out of the harsher realities of 'man's inhumanity to man':

> The Clouds that gather round the setting sun
> *Do take a sober colouring from an eye*
> *That hath kept watch o'er man's mortality.*

By comparison with *Tintern Abbey* and *The Prelude*, we can see that the lyrical form of the Ode, with its varied stanza pattern and melodic rhyme, involves a greater dependence upon imagery than upon argument. The dominant image through which Wordsworth's sense of loss and recovery is expressed is that of light (and its corollary, seeing). The vividness of Wordsworth's early sense impressions is suggested by the idea that, in his youth, everything was 'apparelled in celestial light'. Though he now 'can see no more', there are moments of illumination associated with this celestial light—the sight of a rainbow, or the moon, or a starry night, or the morning sunshine—all reflections of a greater luminosity. Nevertheless, the 'visionary gleam' is fled, 'shades of the prison house' close in around the 'vision splendid', so that it fades 'into the light of common day', becoming finally 'the darkness of the grave' itself. The 'embers' of the divine fire survive in 'shadowy recollections'; but these are precious—the 'fountain-light of all our day', the 'master-light of all our seeing'. Though 'the radiance which was once so bright' is gone and clouds 'gather round the setting sun', their colour, however sober, remains a colour and the 'innocent brightness' of the new-born day is 'lovely yet'.

There are two other major images, those of the sea and flowers. From 'the eternal deep', that 'immortal sea' to whose shores the child alone has access, we have come 'inland' and it is only on the best of days that we can hear its 'mighty waters rolling evermore'. The 'Fresh flowers' culled by children on a May morning are further emblems of this sense of loss and rehabilitation. In moments of exhilaration 'the Rose' is 'lovely' but the pansy at his feet speaks of something that is gone. It also speaks of something partly recovered, for, to the mature Wordsworth,

> . . . the meanest flower that blows can give
> Thoughts that do often lie too deep for tears.

Its fragile beauty is still precious as a token, no longer of immortality, but of the mortality of man.

The Prelude

If the *Immortality Ode* tells us that the child enjoys what adults are toiling all their lives to find, *The Prelude* attempts to capture these things before they can be seen no more, to fetch 'invigorating thoughts from former years'. The design of *The Prelude* does not permit the pattern of the growth of Wordsworth's experience to emerge as simply and clearly as it does in *Tintern Abbey* but, if we take the clearer design of *Tintern Abbey* as our basis, we can see a corresponding pattern emerge in *The Prelude*:

i. The simple physical delight in Nature:

'I held *unconscious intercourse* with beauty
Old as creation, drinking in a *pure*
Organic pleasure . . .

(I, 563–5)

. . . The passion yet
Was *in its birth, sustained* as might befall
By nourishment that came unsought; for still
From week to week, from month to month, we lived
A round of tumult.

(II, 5–8)

ii. The more mystical and spiritual pleasure which followed:

. . . hence, from the same source,
Sublimer joy; for I would walk alone,
Under the quiet stars, and at that time
Have felt whate'er there is of *power* in sound
To breathe an elevated mood.

(II, 301–5)

Thence did I drink *the visionary power;*
And deem not profitless those fleeting moods
Of shadowy exultation.

(II, 311–13)

iii. The love of nature leading to the love of man and the
more sober attitude this change produces:

> . . . in this time
> Of dereliction and dismay, *I yet*
> *Despair not of our nature* . . .
>
> .   .   .   .
>
> . . . and in thee,
> For *this uneasy heart of ours*, I find
> *A never-failing principle of joy*
> *And purest passion*
>
> (II, 440–50)

It is curious that a similar pattern of spiritual growth was
felt by Keats:

> I will return to Wordsworth—whether or no he has
> an extended vision or a circumscribed grandeur—
> whether he is an eagle in his nest, or on the wing—And
> to be more explicit and to show you how tall I stand by
> the giant, I will put down a simile of human life as far
> as I now perceive it; that is, to the point to which I say
> we both have arrived at—Well—I compare human life
> to a large Mansion of Many Apartments, two of which
> I can only describe, the doors of the rest being as yet
> shut upon me. The first we step into we call the infant
> or thoughtless Chamber, in which we remain as long
> as we do not think—We remain there a long while,
> and notwithstanding the doors of the second Chamber
> remain wide open, showing a bright appearance, we
> care not to hasten to it; but are at length imperceptibly
> impelled by the awakening of this thinking principle
> within us—we no sooner get into the second Chamber,
> which I shall call the Chamber of Maiden Thought,
> than we become intoxicated with the light and the

atmosphere, we see nothing but pleasant wonders, and think of delaying there for ever in delight: However among the effects this breathing is father of is that tremendous one of sharpening one's vision into the heart and nature of Man—of convincing one's nerves that the world is full of Misery and Heartbreak, Pain, Sickness and oppression—whereby this Chamber of Maiden-Thought becomes gradually darken'd and at the same time on all sides of it many doors are set open —but all dark—all leading to dark passages—we see not the ballance of good and evil. We are in a Mist. *We* are now in that state—We feel the "burden of the Mystery", To this Point was Wordsworth come, as far as I can conceive when he wrote 'Tintern Abbey' and it seems to me that his Genius is explorative of those dark Passages. Now if we live, and go on thinking, we too shall explore them—he is a Genius and superior ⟨to⟩ us, in so far as he can, more than we, make discoveries, and shed a light in them.[1]

I know of no finer praise of Wordsworth by a fellow-poet nor of a better gloss or commentary on his poetry.

The Prelude also echoes other features of *Tintern Abbey* —the recognition of the unity of all creation:

> . . . great the joy I felt
> Communing in this sort *through earth and heaven*
> *With every form of creature* . . . .
>
> . . . .
>
> *One song they sang*, and it was audible . . .
>
> (II, 410–15)

---

[1] *Letters*, ed. Buxton Forman, p. 143.

the moral effect of natural influences on human behaviour:

> If in my youth I have been *pure in heart*,
> If, mingling with the world, I am *content*
> *With my own modest pleasures*, and have lived
> With God and Nature communing, *removed*
> *From little enmities and low desires*,
> The gift is yours;
>
> > (II, 428–32)

and finally the interaction of the mind with the objects it contemplates through the agency of a power which acts as

> . . . creator and receiver both,
> Working *but in alliance* with the works
> Which it beholds.
>
> > (II, 258–60)

2. *Creative Vision*

It is in this last concept, that of a creative vision, that Wordsworth differs most from his contemporaries. The importance of environment in the development of the child's personality was not original to Wordsworth. The eighteenth-century philosopher David Hartley (1705–57), some of whose ideas coloured those of Coleridge, had stressed the importance of the way in which we associate ideas and therefore of the influences to which we are exposed. He held that men are not born with a moral character already developed but that they acquire it during childhood and adolescence as a product of the physical sensations (pleasure or pain) caused by their experiences. A good illustration of this may be found in Coleridge's poem, *Frost at Midnight*. The poet is addressing his baby son, Hartley (named after the philosopher; he is also, incidentally, the 'Child' of the *Immortality Ode*):

. . . For I was reared
In the great city, pent 'mid cloisters dim,
And saw nought lovely but the sky and stars.
But *thou*, my babe! shall wander like a breeze
By lakes and sandy shores, beneath the crags
Of ancient mountain, and beneath the clouds,
Which image in their bulk both lakes and shores
And mountain crags: so shalt thou see and hear
The lovely shapes and sounds intelligible
Of that eternal language which thy God
Utters, who from eternity doth teach
Himself in all, and all things in himself.[1]

To simple 'sensationalism' of this kind, in which the mind
merely received impressions from outside, Wordsworth
would not subscribe, partly because he believed that the
universe was not mechanical but 'active', but chiefly
because his own experience, as he relates it in the skating
and stolen boat episodes and many other parts of *The
Prelude*, taught him that the human mind was capable of
interpreting this universe in an increasingly meaningful
way. It cannot be too strongly emphasized that, whatever
our difficulty in accepting Wordsworth's beliefs as he
formulates them in *The Prelude*, if we are reading closely
enough to share the experiences which he describes, we
must believe in those experiences as a psychological fact
about Wordsworth (and therefore, perhaps about ourselves?) and also as the prime source of our enjoyment of

---

[1] See also *The Nightingale*. Young Hartley's exposure to life
and letters had, unfortunately, only a moderate success; which
may demonstrate, among other things, the superiority of
Wordsworth's position.

his poetry. It is the incidents which lend conviction to the theory, not the other way round.

The clearest statement of Wordsworth's views is in Book XII:

> This efficacious spirit chiefly lurks
> Among those passages of life that give
> Profoundest knowledge to what point, and how,
> *The mind is lord and master—outward sense*
> *The obedient servant of her will,*
>
> (219–22)

but the same idea occurs in Books I and II. There would seem to be three stages in the process by which the mystical relationship is brought about. First, he begins to be aware of the creative activity of his mind as it operates on what it sees, though at this stage the external images are still predominant:

> . . . *A plastic power*
> Abode *within me*; a *forming hand*, at times
> Rebellious, acting in a devious mood;
> A local spirit of his own, at war,
> With general tendency, but, for the most,
> *Subservient strictly to external things*
> With which it communed.
>
> (II, 362–8)

We should again notice how Wordsworth lends conviction to his argument by the use of particular, sharply-observed images:

> . . . the midnight storm
> Grew darker in the presence of my eye,

just as in the *Immortality Ode*, 'The Clouds that gather

round the setting sun' take on a sober colouring 'from an eye/That hath kept watch o'er man's mortality'.

The second stage appears to be one in which he is aware of images *within* his mind, as if they had passed, through his senses, from an outer to an inner existence:

> Oft in these moments such a holy calm
> Would overspread my soul, that *bodily eyes*
> *Were utterly forgotten,* and what I saw
> *Appeared like something in myself, a dream,*
> *A prospect in the mind.*
>
> (II, 348–52)

In the third stage, the life of the senses is entirely suspended and the poet enters a mystical 'power of joy' in which he sees 'into the life of things', into everything

> . . . that, lost beyond the reach of thought
> And human knowledge, to the human eye
> Invisible, *yet liveth to the heart.*
>
> (II, 403–5)

It is a condition of this deeper awareness that, ironically, those same physical senses which initiate it should have to be in abeyance. The hymn of Nature was most audible says Wordsworth, only

> . . . when the *fleshly ear*
> O'ercome by humblest prelude of that strain,
> Forgot her functions, and slept undisturb,
>
> (II, 416–18)

just as the visionary gleam was brightest when the

> . . . *bodily eyes*
> *Were utterly forgotten,* and what I saw
> Appeared like something in myself.

In Book XII of *The Prelude* he calls the 'bodily' eyes 'The most despotic of the senses'. Sometimes the teeming images of his brain were almost an impediment to clear perception; yet, paradoxically, they were the master-light of all his seeing.

3. *Beauty and Fear*

What are the means by which Nature effects her discipline on the growing boy? They are the occasions she provides for evoking the emotions of pleasure and fear. Wordsworth believed in the free exercise of childhood emotion—he thought that such lack of inhibition would allow the child its best opportunity for finding its own maturity. What he thinks of more 'rational' systems of education he tells us in Book V, and the passage (it is too long to be quoted in full) is interesting because it demonstrates all that a child should *not* be, all that Wordsworth had been spared:

> This model of a child is never known
> To mix in quarrels; that were far beneath
> His dignity . . .
>
> . . . .
>
> He knows the policies of foreign lands;
> Can string you names of districts, cities, towns
> The whole world over, tight as beads of dew
> Upon a gossamer thread . . .
>
> . . . .
>
> For this unnatural growth the trainer blame,
> Pity the tree.
>
> (V, 299–329)

Amid the natural hazards of his boyhood, Wordsworth learned no such theoretical knowledge, but Nature taught him, through experience, three degrees of emotion: unmixed delight, troubled pleasure and pure fright:

> Whether her *fearless visitings*, or those
> That came with *soft alarm*, like hurtless light
> Opening the peaceful clouds; or she may use
> *Severer interventions.*
>
> (I, 352–5)

But this is to theorize; Nature worked, in fact, through the agency of actual 'caves and trees', 'woods and hills' and

> Impressed upon all forms *the characters*
> *Of danger or desire.*
>
> (I, 470–1)

Again, it is in the exemplification of these emotions that the power of the poetry lies and Wordsworth gives many illustrations of all three degrees of feeling. Thus, there was pure delight when he

> Made one long bathing of a summer's day;
> Basked in the sun, and plunged and basked again,

or watched the sun 'lay His beauty on the morning hills'. Sometimes, as when he felt the loud dry wind blow through his ear and the clouds moved with what seemed a cosmic motion, the pleasure of exhilaration would be tempered by the peril of the ridge where he

> . . . hung
> Above the raven's nest, by knots of grass
> And half-inch fissures in the slippery rock.

E

At others there would be, as in the stolen boat episode, a moment of sheer panic when

> . . . from behind that craggy steep till then
> The horizon's bound, a huge peak, black and huge,
> As if with voluntary power instinct
> Upreared its head,

an alarm which persisted for many days and, like so many of his emotions, became an integral part of his personality, as the

> . . . huge and mighty forms, that do not live
> Like living men, moved slowly through the mind

and were a trouble to his dreams.

Such powerful images remain with us all our lives. If they are grand and beautiful enough, as these were, they somehow ennoble the emotions they evoke because these emotions are directed towards images that are normally benign rather than horrific, and normally lofty rather than trivial:

> . . . purifying thus
> The elements of feeling and of thought,
> And *sanctifying, by such discipline,*
> *Both pain and fear,* until we recognize
> A grandeur in the beatings of the heart.
>
> (I, 410–14)

The images must be both natural and sublime; Wordsworth is not advocating either sensationalism or brutality as an aid to spiritual development. He is thinking rather of the element of fear that may exist in such emotions as awe, bewilderment, wonder and, possibly, love. We 'recognize' the grandeur in the heart-beats because it is inherently there; the communion with nature merely reveals it to us as part of our essential self. So,

> By the impressive discipline of fear,
> By pleasure and repeated happiness,
> So frequently repeated, and by force
> Of obscure feelings representative
> Of things forgotten, these same scenes so bright,
> So beautiful, so majestic in themselves,
> Though yet the day was distant, did become
> Habitually dear, and all their forms
> And changeful colours *by invisible links*
> *Were fastened to the affections.*
>
> (I, 603–12)

In W. H. Auden's *The Sea and the Mirror*, the aged Gonzalo realizes that he has overvalued the power of the intellect:

> Since a storm's decision gave
> His subjective passion back
> To a meditative man
> Even reminiscence can
> Comfort ambient troubles like
> Some ruined tower by the sea
> Whence boyhoods growing and afraid
> Learn a formula they need
> In solving their mortality.

Unless I misunderstand it, this seems to be close to what Wordsworth is saying in *The Prelude*. There, *his* formula in solving his mortality lay in the benign influence of natural objects.

4. *Recollected Emotion*

That reminiscence can comfort ambient troubles is an idea that occurs throughout all Wordsworth's writings. We have seen that his own poetry took its origin 'from emotion recollected in tranquillity'. It was not, he tells us in the opening of Book I of *The Prelude*, his habit

> . . . to make
> A present joy the matter of a song.

To Wordsworth, even unpleasant sensations could, as part of a later contemplation, give a kind of pleasure, particularly as part of the process of artistic creation: 'The emotion, of whatever kind, and in whatever degree, from various causes, is qualified by various pleasures so that in describing any passions whatsoever, which are voluntarily described, the mind will, upon the whole, be in a state of enjoyment.' (Preface to the *Lyrical Ballads*.) If this were not so, we may ask ourselves, how should we tolerate a Satan, an Iago or the madness of a Lear? But in *The Prelude* Wordsworth is thinking chiefly of the effect of memory *in his own life* and *The Prelude* itself is a deliberate cultivation of memories in order that they may become permanent:

> —Unfading recollections! at this hour
> The heart is almost mine with which I felt.

That such recollections can bring solace is, of course, the theme of two well-known short poems, 'I wandered lonely as a cloud' and *The Solitary Reaper*. It was Wordsworth's experience that the pattern of these 'Rememberable things' was not clear at the time but that they passed unnoticed into the mind, where they were

. . . doomed to sleep
Until maturer seasons called them forth
To impregnate and to elevate the mind.

(I, 594–6)

The idea is a difficult one to grasp, because Wordsworth
seems to be saying that the matter is not as simple as
remembering something happy when you happen to feel
sad but that, 'Felt in the blood and felt along the heart'
(*Tintern Abbey*), these recollections enter and inform the
total personality of a man so that he becomes tranquil and
has a balanced view of life, as well as an impulse towards
something a little better than himself:

. . . the soul
Remembering *how* she felt, but *what* she felt
Remembering not, retains an obscure sense
Of possible sublimity, whereto
With growing faculties she doth aspire.

(II, 314–18)

That is why, in *The Prelude* and for the remainder of his
days, Wordsworth was

. . . loth to quit
Those recollected hours that have the charm
Of visionary things, those lovely forms
And sweet sensations that throw back our life,
And almost make remotest infancy
A visible scene, on which the sun is shining.

(II, 630–5)

Some questions:

1. Trace the ways in which Wordsworth was 'disci-
plined' by beauty and fear.

2. To what extent is sympathy with Wordsworth's views a necessary part of the appreciation of his poetry?

3. How successful is Wordsworth in integrating the various strands of thought and feeling in the first two books of *The Prelude*? Is it possible to separate the 'philosophy' from the 'experience'?

4. 'All Wordsworth's poetry consists of variations on the theme of *Tintern Abbey*.' Comment on this observation in relation to *The Prelude*, Books I and II, and any other poetry of Wordsworth you have read.

5. Keats disliked 'poetry that has a palpable design on us'. Is his phrase applicable to Books I and II of *The Prelude*?

Suggested readings:

Wordsworth: *Tintern Abbey* and *Immortality Ode*;
Miscellaneous lyrics: 'I wandered lonely as a cloud'; 'Strange fits of passion have I known'; 'A slumber did my spirit seal'; 'My heart leaps up'; *The Solitary Reaper*.
Coleridge: *Frost at Midnight*; *The Nightingale*.
Dylan Thomas: *Fern Hill; The Force that through the Green Fuse Drives the Flower*.

SOME INCIDENTS

It is rather fashionable today to distinguish between the genuine quality of Wordsworth's experiences and the unacceptability of the beliefs which he draws from them. In selecting for discussion some of the incidents in which those experiences are embodied, I do not wish to appear to be suggesting agreement with this distinction; I think it is possible to see that each episode fits into a complex interweaving of sensation and thought, in the design of the poem as a whole. At the same time, it is clear that *sensation* comes first. If we do not believe in Wordsworth's experiences, then we cannot accept what he has to say about those experiences; they are, in fact, the justification of his poem.

His method, if that is the right word, is to trace the growth of an experience with such particularity that he re-creates in the reader the emotional state of the boy who is living it, so that the reader himself, in the process of sharing the experience, learns something of Wordsworth's feeling of intimacy with natural objects and follows the growth of the poet's mind.

I wish now to look at three incidents from Book I— snaring, bird-nesting and the stolen boat (the skating passage is discussed more fully on page 78, but it illustrates the same points and should be borne in mind). It is interesting, I think, that all demonstrate a similar pattern of experience, in which the boy is stimulated, by suspense or by sudden fear, into an increased awareness of his surroundings and hence into a visionary state; in each there is a period of intense concentration, accompanied by faint feelings of guilt, followed by a kind of relaxation in which the former object of contemplation is replaced with startling vividness by a new perception associated with it. We know this to have been a common occurrence with Wordsworth. It is the theme of 'Strange fits of passion', and Wordsworth told de Quincey:

I have remarked, from my earliest days, that if the attention is energetically braced up to an act of steady observation, or of steady expectation, then if this intense condition of vigilance should suddenly relax, at that moment any beautiful, any impressive visual object falling upon the eye, is carried to the heart with a power not known under other circumstances. Just now my ear was placed upon the stretch, in order to catch any sound of wheels that might come down from the Keswick Road; at the very instant when I raised my head from the ground, in final abandonment of hope for this night, when the organs of attention were all at once relaxing, the bright star hanging in the air above those outlines of massy blackness fell suddenly upon my eye, and penetrated my capacity of apprehension with a pathos and a sense of the infinite that would not have arrested me under other circumstances.

But there are many other common elements in the passages. In each the scene is set as one of great natural beauty and clarity—in 'the breath of frosty wind', the clear air of the 'high places' above the cultured Vale or the cloudless moonlit night with the water 'glittering idly'. Sound and colour and naturalistic detail lend conviction to the scene and root it in reality—the wind 'had snapped the last autumnal crocus'; the poet hung 'by

knots of grass/And half-inch fissures in the slippery rock';
the reflected moonlight 'melted all into one track/Of
sparkling light'; the boat may be an 'elfin pinnace' but it
is tied to a very real willow with a very real chain.

In each passage, too, the feeling of immediacy is
sustained by the use of present participles (or nouns and
adjectives deriving from them). These assist the reader's
participation in events otherwise related in the past tense
so that he is induced to follow the experience in the
telling, rather than to regard it as something already
completed: scudding; wanderings; breathings; shoulder-
ing; stepping; glittering; sparkling; unswerving; hearing;
growing; living; trembling; being.

On each occasion the boy is alone (this is stated in the
first two passages and implied in the third) and, before the
climax of the scene, he has been indulging in vigorous
movement: 'let loose/For sports of wider range', ranging
'the open heights', 'Scudding away from snare to snare';
roving as a plunderer, hanging 'above the raven's nest';
lustily dipping his oars 'into the silent lake' and rising
upon each stroke.

In each case, too, the boy is actively pursuing some
object of desire which he acknowledges to be partly illicit:
'a strong desire/O'erpowered my better reason'; he is a
plunderer, 'mean our object and inglorious'; 'it was an act
of stealth/And troubled pleasure'. Some of the energy and
movement which he devotes to this pursuit is transferred
to natural objects: the sound of his breath and the echo
of his footsteps seem to come from 'the solitary hills',
his giddiness 'moved the clouds' with a strange motion,
the regular stroke of his panic-stricken oars becomes the
'measured motion' of the craggy peak.

This leads to an identification with natural objects

which is part of his experience of intercourse with Nature:
he scuds 'Along the smooth green turf' like the woodcocks;
he is 'suspended by the blast' which blows around the
crags; as he rose upon each stroke, his boat 'Went heaving
through the water like a swan'.

Before each climax his whole energy is concentrated
on one object: 'Through half the night' he plied 'that
anxious visitation'; his whole sense of self-preservation
goes to keep him 'but ill sustained' on his half-inch
fissure in the rock; he fixed his view 'upon the summit
of a craggy ridge' so that he would 'reach a chosen point.'

Finally, at the climax of each incident he undergoes a
mystical, trance-like experience:

> I heard among the solitary hills
> Low breathings coming after me, and sounds
> Of undistinguishable motion, steps,
> Almost as silent as the turf they trod.
>
> With what strange utterance did the loud dry wind
> Blow through my ear! the sky seemed not a sky
> Of earth—and with what motion moved the clouds.
>
> . . . huge and mighty forms, that do not live
> Like living men, moved slowly through the mind
> By day, and were a trouble to my dreams.

Of course we can find naturalistic explanations of these
experiences. Wordsworth is transferring his concentration
and feeling of guilt to inanimate, non-moral things and
investing them with a moral quality, and we can say, if we
wish, that the low breathings and the footsteps were his
own and that the clouds moved strangely because he was
suffering from vertigo. We can even draw a simple diagram

to show how, as he rowed away from it, Black Crag became
more clearly visible behind Styebarrow. But this is to
miss the point, which is that to Wordsworth the crag
seemed to be following him; as the reader follows the
experience it *seems* to be true to him, too, and thus
becomes a fact of his own mind.

There are two episodes in Book II (lines 115–30 and
161–74) in which Wordsworth's soul is fostered by beauty
rather than by fear. These record a slightly different
experience, that of a suspension of the physical world in a
moment of great calm. It is perhaps significant that they
occur when Wordsworth was a little older. Wordsworth
has also recorded this sensation elsewhere:

> There was a time in my life when I was often forced
> to grasp, like this, something that existed, to be sure
> that there was anything outside of me. This gate, this
> bar, this road, these trees fell away from me and vanished
> into thought. I was sure of the existence of my mind—
> I had no sense of the existence of matter.

The pattern of these two incidents is simpler—a period of
noisy, violent exercise is followed by a moment of intense
peace. First there is vigorous movement:

> Our steeds remounted and the summons given,
> With whip and spur we through the chantry flew.

> . . . through half an afternoon we played
> On the smooth platform, whether skill prevailed
> Or happy blunder triumphed, bursts of glee
> Made all the mountains ring;

then a sudden substitution of this communal revelry by an individual note:

> . . . that single wren
> Which one day sang so sweetly in the nave.

The Minstrel of the Troop. . . ./Alone upon the rock.

The resulting emotion in each case is brought about by a musical sound:

> . . . I could have made
> My dwelling-place and lived for ever there
> To hear such music;
> . . . and left him there
> And rowed off gently, while he blew his flute.

It produces a calm which

> . . . sank down
> Into my heart and held me like a dream.

When Wordsworth tells us that he was 'Fostered alike by beauty and by fear', he does not ask us to take him on trust. In passages like these he presents his credentials.

Some questions:

1. 'The success of *The Prelude* depends upon genuine personal experience being available to validate, by its work upon the reader, what otherwise would be a series of empty assertions'. Comment on this observation in relation to Books I and II.

2. How true is it that Wordsworth's view of Nature is a limited one, based on his happy life in the Lake District? Would his views have been different had he lived in Equatorial Africa?

3. Is there any reason to suppose that an autobiographical novel would have been more suited to Wordsworth's purposes?

4. Relate the skating episode to the others which are discussed in this chapter.

Suggested reading:

Wordsworth: *The Prelude*, Book VI, lines 557–616; Book XII, lines 208–335; *A Guide through the District of the Lakes*.

STYLE

In talking about the 'style' of a poem we must be careful not to regard it as an isolated aspect of composition, as if it were something added, in an ornamental fashion, to what has already been arrived at in some other way. We should try to see it as an integral part of what the poet is saying, as affecting, and also controlling, his *meaning* as well as his *expression*. All poetry is, of course, an affair of meaningful words so that this is bound to be a question of degree. Wordsworth presents an especially difficult case for discussion because his poetry has few of the qualities that lend themselves to the fashionable analytical techniques which seize so readily on the interplay of metaphor, irony and other forms of figurative language. It is Wordsworth's peculiar genius to distil from an incident a particular emotion and then to find words which will convey the quality of that emotion as accurately as possible:

Made one long bathing of a summer's day.

The easily observable elements of Wordsworth's poetry are not many and not readily distinguishable from the context in which they occur. Before proceeding to any generalizations about his style, therefore, let us examine in detail the skating episode from Book I, where all these elements may been seen working together.

1. *'Culpably Particular'* (Book I, lines 425–63)

And in the frosty season, when the sun
Was set, and visible for many a mile
The cottage windows blazed through twilight gloom,

I heeded not their summons: happy time
It was indeed for all of us—for me
It was a time of rapture! Clear and loud
The village clock tolled six,—I wheeled about,
Proud and exulting like an untired horse
That cares not for his home. All shod with steel,
We hissed along the polished ice in games
Confederate, imitative of the chase
And woodland pleasures,—the resounding horn,
The pack loud chiming, and the hunted hare.
So through the darkness and the cold we flew,
And not a voice was idle; with the din
Smitten, the precipices rang aloud;
The leafless trees and every icy crag
Tinkled like iron; while far distant hills
Into the tumult sent an alien sound
Of melancholy not unnoticed, while the stars
Eastward were sparkling clear, and in the west
The orange sky of evening died away.
Not seldom from the uproar I retired
Into a silent bay, or sportively
Glanced sideway, leaving the tumultuous throng,
To cut across the reflex of a star
That fled, and, flying still before me, gleamed
Upon the glassy plain; and oftentimes
When we had given our bodies to the wind,
And all the shadowy banks on either side
Came sweeping through the darkness, spinning still
The rapid line of motion, then at once
Have I, reclining back upon my heels,
Stopped short; yet still the solitary cliffs
Wheeled by me—even as if the earth had rolled
With visible motion her diurnal round!

> Behind me did they stretch in solemn train,
> Feebler and feebler, and I stood and watched
> Till all was tranquil as a dreamless sleep.

Like the other passages which end in a visionary experience, this one begins in circumstances of great visual clarity; the season is 'frosty' and the cottage windows are 'visible for many a mile'. Characteristically, Wordsworth 'heeded not their summons' and this helps to underline his preference for 'natural' rather than 'domestic' intercourse. He is not yet alone—it was a happy time 'for all of us'—but he is nevertheless marked out from his fellows by his heightened organic and spiritual sensibility: '*for me*,/It was a time of *rapture*!'; the verse quickens to catch the mood of exhilaration. Not only are some things clearly visible even in the twilight gloom but the frosty air makes others audible with especial clarity: 'Clear and loud/ The village clock tolled six.' Again the quality of the verse shifts slightly, to accommodate the successive sounds: 'hissed', 'resounding horn', 'the pack loud chiming'; and to adjust itself to the swift animal vitality:

> . . . I wheeled about,
> Proud and exulting like an untired horse.

Like the horse, he, too, is 'shod with steel'. The long vowel-sound of 'wheeled' captures the arc of Wordsworth's turning movement and the repetition of sounds in ab*ou*t/ Pr*ou*d suggests the pause and plunge of the returning arc. The alliteration of the letter 's' imitates, in splendid onomatopoeia, the *sound* of skating, as surely as the repetition of the letter 'i' does its swift, clean *movement*:

> . . . All *s*hod wi*t*h *s*teel,
> We hi*ss*ed along the poli*s*hed *i*ce *i*n game*s*.

The hard, cold feeling suggested by the steel is sustained

by a number of words which echo clear metallic sounds: 'chiming', 'smitten', 'rang', 'tinkled like iron'. The scene is one of noisy exuberance, like those we have looked at in Book II—'not a voice was idle'—but again there strikes across the scene a melancholy note, not this time an actual sound, unless this is the answering echo of the hills:

> . . . while far distant hills
> Into the tumult sent an alien sound
> Of melancholy not unnoticed.

The hills are far distant; they represent something outside the small, happy world they enclose. Wordsworth is not unmindful of them but, as yet, their alien sound is something he has still to contend with, something outside the scope of his boyhood experience—the 'still, sad music of humanity'. Is it this which distinguishes him from the others? At any rate, he retires 'Not seldom from the uproar . . . Into a silent bay', as his poetic calling will later mark him off from his fellow men. By now the orange sky of evening has died away, withdrawing the colour from the scene and prefiguring the 'dreamless sleep' of the last line. Alone, Wordsworth pursues the image of a star which 'gleams' in startling actuality upon a 'glassy' plain to remind us that, whatever its metaphorical overtones, this was a real image of an actual star. Since, however, it is a reflection, it recedes, as he pursues it with the concentration and desire we have noticed in the other episodes, so that a close identification of the boy, the star and the image is produced in the reader's mind. Is this an emblem of the experience he is to record in Book II:

> With faculties still growing, feeling still
> That whatsoever point they gain, they yet
> Have something to pursue?

F

Wordsworth's choice of the word 'reflex' permits him a terminal letter 'x' which has the curious and subtle function of suggesting, by its shape, three possible effects: an image and its reflection, the form of a star and the intersection of the skater's tracks. The sound of '*c*ut *across* the refle*x*' captures the bite of the skate in the ice. A further identification with nature is made as they give their bodies 'to the wind' and the transfer of movement that we have noticed elsewhere also takes place here, for it is the banks which seem to be 'sweeping through the darkness', not the skater. The movement is very fast:

> . . . spinning still
> The rapid line of motion, then at once
> Have I, reclining back upon my heels
> Stopped short;

but comes abruptly to a halt on the two monosyllables, while at the same time contriving to continue its own momentum through the remainder of the line:

> . . . yet still the solitary cliffs
> Wheeled by me—even as if the earth had rolled
> With visible motion her diurnal round!

so that Wordsworth brings off an uncanny sensation of simultaneous stillness and movement. In an increasing series of turning concentric circles, the 'spinning' of the skater becomes the 'wheeling' of the cliffs and then the slower 'rolling' of the earth. We can believe in this 'visible motion' because we have already 'seen' the wheeling of the skater's arc-like turn, and the identification of the boy and the turning world is underlined by the solitariness of both the boy and the cliffs. Even the slow and ponderous 'd*i*urnal', with its turning double vowel, supported by the vowels of 'rolled', 'motion' and 'round', produces an additional effect by suggesting something grander and more mysterious than the simple 'daily' round. The infinite recession of the hills, growing 'feebler and feebler', as the images recede from his bodily eye and the effect of giddiness is replaced by a trance-like calm, stretches out into the silent night and the farther reaches of experience that the night implies.

Again, as with the other episodes it resembles, it would be possible to find a naturalistic explanation. We could say, simply, that he felt dizzy. But to Wordsworth it seemed that he had felt the turning world and was part of it; if we read closely, we can share his conviction.

2. 'A More Exact Notion'

Anyone who attempts to write about Wordsworth's style must echo a sentiment expressed by Wordsworth himself in the Preface to the *Lyrical Ballads*:

> Without being culpably particular, I do not know how to give my Reader a more exact notion of the style in which it was my wish and intention to write than by informing him that I have at all times endeavoured to look steadily at my subject.

To look steadily at your subject would seem to suggest that perhaps there are some things which are too important to be left to art, or at least to artifice. Because he was 'a man speaking to men', Wordsworth felt that he could no longer take advantage of a position in which, by regarding his art as to some extent a special craft or 'mystery', the poet could become partly detached from his poem, shaping it with conscious care. One result of this attitude is that his poetry is largely autobiographical; another is that its stylistic features are likely to be the accidental results of his meaning rather than deliberate aids to expression; yet another is a tendency to call a spade a spade (in fact, to address a poem to one.) We should not therefore expect to find in his poetry far-fetched conceits in the manner of the Metaphysical poets or elaborate use of rhetorical devices. Another kind of artificiality—the use of outworn 'phrases and figures of speech which from father to son have long been regarded as the common inheritance of Poets'—he objects to in the work of Gray. In the Preface to *Lyrical Ballads* he printed the following sonnet of Gray, with some lines in italics:

> In vain to me the smiling mornings shine,
> And reddening Phoebus lifts his golden fire:
> The birds in vain their amorous descant join,
> Or cheerful fields resume their green attire.
> These ears, alas! for other notes repine;
> *A different object do these eyes require;*
> *My lonely anguish melts no heart but mine;*
> *And in my breast the imperfect joys expire;*
> Yet morning smiles the busy race to cheer,
> And new-born pleasure brings to happier men;
> The fields to all their wonted tribute bear;
> To warm their little loves the birds complain.
> *I fruitless mourn to him that cannot hear,*
> *And weep the more because I weep in vain.*

(It is interesting to compare this with Wordsworth's own

sonnet on a similar theme, 'Surprised by joy . . .') Wordsworth commented on Gray's poem, 'The only part of this
sonnet which is of any value is the lines printed in italics.'
We can see why; not merely because 'the language of
these lines does in no respect differ from that of prose',
which is the reason Wordsworth gives (a not very satis-
factory reason because it begs more questions than it
answers) but chiefly because the lines *seem* to lack artifice,
to be the sincere, natural, unforced and, above all, uncon-
cealed expression of emotion.

Wordsworth's verdict is biased, of course, and it is not
a very perceptive one, as we can see today. He has, in fact,
missed the point—that the effect of Gray's poem depends
to a large extent upon the contrast between conventionally
impersonal expressions of happiness and deeply-felt
personal expressions of grief, and that, even in the lines
which he italicises, the balancing effect of antithesis
carries a large expressive weight: 'lonely anguish/imperfect
joys; 'I weep the more/I weep in vain'.

But Gray was a very good poet, even if possibly a minor
one, as we can judge from this distance. A lot of minor
eighteenth century poetry is by no means of this calibre,
though it may imitate its outward features; to Wordsworth, at the time, it must have seemed that he was
clearing away a good deal of undergrowth, as indeed he
was. The blank verse of *The Prelude* (a ten-syllable line
of three or four irregular stresses) may lead the poet away
from some of the devices he might be tempted into by
rhyming poetry, but it presents its own kind of difficulty,
as Wordsworth tells us:

> Dr. Johnson observed, that in blank verse, the
> language suffered more distortion to keep it out of

prose than any inconvenience to be apprehended
from the shackles and circumspection of rhyme.
This kind of distortion is the worst fault that poetry
can have; for if once the natural order and connection of the words is broken, and the idiom of the
language violated, the lines appear manufactured,
and lose all that character of enthusiasm and
inspiration, without which they become cold and
insipid, how sublime soever the ideas and the images
may be which they express.

We can see that Wordsworth equates the genuine and
sincere with the artless and uncontrived. It is not an
equation that holds good for all poetry (Pope's intense
moral commitment depends to an extent on certain
stylistic habits) or even for all Wordsworth's poetry, as we
know from his repeated alterations to *The Prelude*; but
it is valid for a good deal of it. The points which follow
should be seen, therefore, as incidental features of Wordsworth's style, *belonging* to what he wants to say, but
arising from it rather than simply *contributing to* it.

Since we have examined a descriptive extract in detail,
it may be useful to look at a passage connected with it but
differing from it—the invocation to the 'Wisdom and
Spirit of the Universe' (I, lines 401–24) which precedes
the skating episode:

> Wisdom and Spirit of the universe!
> Thou soul that art the eternity of thought,
> That givest to forms and images a breath
> And everlasting motion, not in vain
> By day or star-light thus from my first dawn
> Of childhood didst thou intertwine for me
> The passions that build up our human soul;

Not with the mean and vulgar works of man,
But with high objects, with enduring things—
With life and nature—purifying thus
The elements of feeling and of thought,
And sanctifying, by such discipline,
Both pain and fear, until we recognise
A grandeur in the beatings of the heart.
Nor was this fellowship vouchsafed to me
With stinted kindness.

One feature which clearly defines it is a negative one—
it lacks both the characteristic Shakespearean quality of
shifting metaphor (cf. Macbeth's 'Tomorrow and tomorrow and tomorrow . . .' soliloquy) or the Miltonic one of
the emphatic placing of key words, sometimes of opposite
meaning (cf. any of Satan's speeches in *Paradise Lost*).
With one exception—'dawn' (not very noticeable because
of its association in the same line with 'day' and 'starlight', both used literally)—there is little obvious metaphor.
'Kindness' is an extension of the personification of the
Spirit, as is, possibly, 'breath'; 'purifying' and 'sanctifying', while taken from a religious context, have here for
Wordsworth an almost literal meaning. After the opening
two lines, most of the others are 'run-on'; that is, the sense
of the passage does not come to a halt at the end of each
line but flows into the next without pause. This assists
the feeling that the words are not deliberately placed but
fall naturally into their right position without drawing
attention to themselves. This in turn contributes to an
impression of sincerity and conviction. The 'distortion' to
which Wordsworth objected is here noticeable only in the
form of the occasional inversion of subject and verb or the
positioning of an adverbial phrase: 'not in vain . . . didst

thou intertwine'; 'Mine was it.' The partial inversion 'was this . . . vouchsafed' follows idiomatically from the use of the conjunction 'Nor' in place of 'And . . . not.'

Other stylistic features tend to be suppressed by the rolling, forward movement of the verse but there are some interesting characteristics. The antithesis of words which we have seen in Gray's sonnet is present here, too, in a less emphatic way. 'Wisdom' and 'Spirit' are picked up in an inverted form in the following line by 'Soul' and 'thought', a cross reference which partially obliterates the distinction between them. There is also present in the following group a complex pattern of cross-reference: 'high objects/ enduring things; life/nature; feeling/thought; pain/fear'. Another noticeable feature is the accumulation of nouns, frequently of an abstract kind, so that the passage becomes very weighty in terms of general ideas. Sometimes these nouns are linked by the preposition 'of', suggesting the closer inter-connection and even identity of the words in question: 'Wisdom (of the Universe); Spirit of the Universe; eternity of thought; dawn of childhood; mean and vulgar works of men; elements of feeling and (elements of) thought; beatings of the heart.' At other times they are linked in pairs by 'and/or' to suggest, not identity, but a range of large inclusiveness, taking in the full spectrum of any idea or possibility: 'Wisdom *and* Spirit; forms *and* images; breath *and* everlasting motion; By day *or* starlight; In November days . . . *and* summer nights; both day *and* night; life *and* nature; of feeling *and* of thought; both pain *and* fear.' In this way Wordsworth is able to suggest that every possible case is caught in the mesh of his verse and thus to assist the demonstration of the unity of all nature and experience which is the aim of the passage. Such large inclusiveness, however magnificently expressed, might not carry much weight if it were not borne out in some other way by the rest of the poem. Four key words, therefore, refer us to incidents which precede this passage: 'images', 'forms', 'motions', and 'breath'. In each case *an earlier precise context* for the word removes the feeling that Wordsworth is indulging in airy generalization:

> . . . No familiar shapes
> Remained, no pleasant *images* of trees,
> Of sea or sky, no colours of green fields;
> But huge and mighty *forms*, that do not live
> Like living men, *moved* slowly through the mind . . .

> . . . with purpose of its own
> And measured *motion* like a living thing
> Strode after me.

> . . . the sky seemed not a sky
> Of earth—and with what *motion* moved the clouds!

> I heard among the solitary hills
> Low *breathings* coming after me, and sounds
> Of undistinguishable *motion* . . .

> I cannot miss my way. I *breathe* again!

> For I, methought, while the sweet *breath* of heaven
> Was blowing on my body, felt within
> *A correspondent breeze.*

The passage will also pass another of Wordsworth's poetical tests—that its language should not differ essentially from that of prose. With the possible exception of 'vouchsafed' there are no words which strike the reader as belonging especially to the sphere of poetry. The elevated tone of the passage is produced partly by the use of quasi-religious terms like 'purifying' and 'sanctifying' but also by the archaic use of a semi-biblical register: 'thou . . . art', 'that givest', 'didst thou', a form normally associated by most of us with the Prayer-book.

The range of Wordsworth's expression can be judged, however, by the adjustment of this exalted tone and manner to meet the needs of a more autobiographical passage beginning at line 416:

> . . . In November days,
> When vapours rolling down the valley made
> A lonely scene more lonesome, among woods,
> At noon and 'mid the calm of summer nights,
> When, by the margin of the trembling lake,
> Beneath the gloomy hills homeward I went
> In solitude, such intercourse was mine;
> Mine was it in the fields both day and night,
> And by the waters, all the summer long.

Here Wordsworth is trying to authenticate what he has just been saying by establishing occasions on which these general truths were made plain to him. The passage is subtly but intensively compounded of alliterative and onomatopoeic effects; one needs to be 'culpably particular' in order to discover them. First we may notice the drowsy, soporific effect of the repeated 'v' and 'm' sounds, alternating with the liquid sound of 'l' to produce a trance-like, lake-side experience: No*v*e*m*ber, *v*aporous, ro*ll*ing, *v*a*ll*ey, *l*one*l*y, *m*ore, *l*oneso*m*e, a*m*ong, *m*id, ca*lm*, su*mm*er, *m*argin, tre*m*b*l*ing *l*ake, g*l*oo*m*y hi*ll*s, ho*m*eward, a*ll* the su*mm*er *l*ong. Then there is the quiet, faintly mystical sensation produced by the long 'a' and 'o' vowel-sounds (contrast lines 439–42 which follow this passage); days, vapours, made, lake, day; November, rolling, lonely, lonesome, homeward, both; woods, noon, gloomy; and by the partial internal rhyme: November/trembling; calm/margin; gloomy/homeward. The interaction of these elements is very complex, as can be seen by the recurrence of most of the words under several headings. In the last resort, the magic is, quite rightly, beyond our analysis.

One of the characteristics of poetry which marks it out as a special mode of expression is its reliance upon metaphor to fuse together ideas not otherwise connected logically. In Shakespeare, this frequently means referring away from the subject to an image almost totally unrelated, so that we see the relationship in a new and startling light and are forced to reconsider our view of both. In Wordsworth, this is rare; the metaphorical activity is subordinated to the general movement and intention of his poem. It is, nevertheless, present and quietly reinforces the other effects of the poetry, but usually it is drawn from sources in nature; that is, it directs attention *towards* the actual subject matter of the poem rather than away from it; the metaphors are either used literally elsewhere in the poem or could be so used without any sense of strain. The following examples are not intended to be exclusive or exhaustive but merely pointers to further study: 'a correspondent breeze' (I, 35), cf. 'like a tempest' (I, 584), for joy and creative activity; 'a long-continued frost' (I, 40) for the inhibition of that activity; 'spring-tide swellings' for the false starts and 'regular sea' for the real accomplishment (I, 167); 'seed-time' (I, 301) for his boyhood and 'transplanted' (I, 305) to suggested the continued growth; 'hurtless light/Opening the peaceful clouds' (I, 353) for the gentle awakening of conscience (this is actually a simile); 'Planting snowdrops among winter snows' (I, 615) for the half-invention of pre-conscious memories; 'The chamois' sinews and the eagle's wing' (II, 275) for the energy and soaring flight of poetic activity.

Sometimes a sequence of religious metaphors will contribute to the feeling of poetic dedication and exalted calling: 'punctual service'; 'Matins and vespers'; 'priestly robe'; 'holy service' (I, 44–54). At others, sensory metaphors denote either the unconscious absorption of natural influences: '*drinking* in a pure/Organic pleasure' (I, 563); '*Drinks* in the feelings of his Mother's eye' (II, 237) (notice how this image picks up the literal association of 'Rocked on his Mother's breast' of the previous line) or the conscious transformation of those influences by the personality of the beholder: 'A *plastic* power/Abode within me; a *forming hand*.' (II, 362).

There is a tendency for most of us today to read all long works of imaginative literature as if they were novels, forgetting that poetry (and poetic drama) can achieve an expressive intensity much greater than that which might be attained by prose works of corresponding length. In the case of Wordsworth, the means by which this intensity is achieved is especially elusive. I have tried above to suggest some possible ways in which the complex effect is produced. In doing so I do not wish to imply that these characteristic features of his poetry were consciously in Wordsworth's mind as he wrote. To indicate their presence in the poem is simply to acknowledge their existence as part of what we mean by 'great poetry'. This is one aspect of the work of criticism but it comes a long way behind the achievement of art. As Wordsworth would say, we murder to dissect.

The vexed question of Wordsworth's religious beliefs
is too large for our present scope; it would lead us to a
consideration of *The Excursion* and of the repeated alterations made to *The Prelude* in the light of Wordsworth's
later orthodoxy. For most readers, the source of their
delight in Wordsworth's poetry comes not from any
systematic ethical philosophy but from his joy in Nature
and, in Matthew Arnold's words, 'the extraordinary
power with which, in case after case, he shows us this joy,
and renders it so as to make us share it'. Neither time nor
changing belief will affect our enjoyment of the essential
Wordsworth. He remains what, as he says, he always was:

> The transitory Being who beheld
> This Vision,

and who tried, 'through sad incompetence of human
speech', to communicate it to others.

Some questions:

1. Make a detailed examination of one of the other
incidents.

2. What differences in style can you detect between
passages of description and passages of reflection?

3. Compare a passage of Wordsworth's blank verse
with one by Milton and one by Shakespeare (say, the
description of Eden in Book IV of *Paradise Lost* and either
John of Gaunt's speech in *Richard II* or Ulysses' speech,
'Time hath, my lord, a wallet at his back . . .' in *Troilus
and Cressida*.)

4. How true is it that the style changes with the needs
of Wordsworth's narrative?

5. If you have access to a copy of *The Prelude* of 1805,

discuss any alterations to that text made for the 1850 version. (The text of Books I and II edited by Helen Darbishire prints occasional extracts from the earlier version.)

Suggested reading:

Wordsworth: Preface to the *Lyrical Ballads* (2nd edition).
Coleridge: *Biographia Literaria*: Chaps. 17 and 22.

General reading:

The standard life is: Mary Moorman: *William Wordsworth. The Early Years; Wordsworth's Later Years.* (O.U.P.) For students new to Wordsworth the best introduction is that by Margaret Drabble: *Wordsworth.* (Evans). Helen Darbishire's *The Poet Wordsworth* (O.U.P.) is a classic study, brief and full of perception, while J. C. Smith's *A Study of Wordsworth* is also short and has an unusual arrangement of material. Advanced students should find stimulating: E. N. W. Bateson: *Wordsworth. A Reinterpretation*, (Longmans) and Sir Herbert Read: *Wordsworth* (Faber).